Centre for Insurance Studies

Seventh Annual PMI Conference

The Proceedings of the Conference *Cutbacks and the New Economic Climate*, held on 31 October, 2002 at the Smurfit Graduate School of Business, University College Dublin.

The Proceedings of this Conference, so far as possible, have been reviewed and where necessary revised and updated by individual contributors. However, the opinions and views expressed are those of the individual participants alone, and not necessarily those of the Centre for Insurance Studies.

The Editor wishes to record his deep appreciation
for the continued support of
Irish Life & Permanent plc
for the work of the Centre for Insurance Studies.
Without their support, this book,
which is so important for every citizen of Ireland,
would not have been published.

CONTENTS

Dedication

Htori Semnoi

"To the Magnanimous Heart"

Ita

Dr Padraic O'Domhnaill   Professor Brian Keogh

Thanks and blessings to all our friends in the health service for their contributions to this book.

Acknowledgements

This book contains the edited contributions of participants at the 2002/2003 Private Medical Insurance (PMI) Conference, *Acute Healthcare in Transition in Ireland: Change, Cutbacks and Challenges*, which was held at the Smurfit Graduate School of Business. A number of additional papers have been included because of their relevance, and the insights they provide into the acute sector, going forward.

I would like to record, with thanks, all of those who supported and helped organise and manage this Conference. Particular thanks are due to David Christopher BA, Hilary Coates SRN, Professor Louis Murray, Edward Shaw MBA, Patricia Dunne and Deirdre Hegarty.

The Conference is one of the key events initiated and developed by the Centre for Insurance Studies (http://www.insurancestudies.org). Its seven Conferences to date on healthcare practice and policy have brought together both Irish and international experts in healthcare insurance in dialogue with key medical, policy and management stakeholders, within the acute sector.

Within the framework of the conference, we have introduced a major innovation, the *St. Raphael's Cup for Distinguished Service to Irish Healthcare*. Its objective is to acknowledge, in a tangible manner, the enormous contribution of individuals and organisations to the provision of healthcare in Ireland, now and over the years. Previous recipients have included the Sisters of Charity, the Hospice Movement and, in 2002, Sr Consilio, for her work in the rehabilitation of alcoholics and, more recently, young people suffering from substance abuse (acknowledged *in absentia*, and subsequently at a reception in Áras an Uachtaráin, by the President of Ireland, Mary McAleese.

Finally, to all of the speakers and participants over the years, to Ruaraí and Porkodi, and to all who have helped along the way, *go raibh míle maith agaibh.*

Ray Kinsella

I

KEY ISSUES RELATING TO ACUTE HEALTHCARE IN IRELAND – AN OVERVIEW

PROFESSOR RAY KINSELLA

DIRECTOR, CENTRE FOR INSURANCE STUDIES, GRADUATE SCHOOL OF BUSINESS, UNIVERSITY COLLEGE DUBLIN

This book brings together contributions from a wide range of experts – clinicians and medical practitioners, policy-makers as well as those involved in management, administration and research – to discuss the present status of, and prospective future developments in, acute care. An integrated practitioner-based analysis of a – perhaps, *the* – core social and political priority is particularly timely. There is, on the one hand, evidence of enormous strains, and also "cutbacks" within the acute system. At the same time, since the publication by Government of the "Health Strategy" (2001), there has been an unprecedented number of policy Reports, as well as strategies in different specialisms. These are indicative of a prospective paradigm shift in the structure, as well as the organisation and delivery, of acute care. The reality, however, is that we are at present in the interregnum: the transition from a deeply inequitable and structurally flawed system to one that is both equitable[1] and ethically-based, as well as financially sustainable, has not yet begun.

The purpose of this Introduction is two-fold. First, it seeks to contextualise the different contributions by providing a brief review of recent policy initiatives. The focus is primarily on the Health Reform Programme (2003), which sets out policy proposals in the field of institutional and management changes in the acute system as well as in the whole area of medical manpower and staffing. Second, the Introduction seeks to provide a "flavour" of the issues raised in different contributions, under a number of headings: namely, key themes, "change-drivers" and major challenges. The individual chapters need to be read, in their entirety, to appreciate the expert – and often robust – arguments being made. At the same time, a necessarily selective overview of the different chapters may be helpful in "setting the scene".

---

[1] See for example, *Equity of Access to Hospital Care: National Economic and Social Forum* (Report Number 25, 2002).

PART I: THE POLICY CONTEXT
I.I.

In June 2003, the Minister for Health and Children set out a Health Reform Programme. It draws – directly or indirectly – on a number of key reports[2]. These dealt, *inter alia*, with Value for Money (VPM), structures and functions within the health service with the aim of reducing fragmentation, enhancing financial performance through increased accountability and strengthening corporate governance. In the critically important field of medical manpower, the Programme drew on the Report of the National Task Force on Medical Staffing (the Hanly Report), dated June 2003 but which was published in October 2003.

There are two basic strands running through the Reform Programme and they resonate of the key issues addressed in the succeeding chapters of this book. The first strand deals with institutional and management reform; the second with the reform of A&E services, the provision of Consultant-delivered services as well as important related issues including education and training.

I.2 INSTITUTIONAL REFORM [3]

The elements of this first strand included proposal to:

- Restructure the Department of Health and Children (DoHC), with a clear separation of executive and non-executive functions. The focus of the Department, it is proposed, is to be on policy development and, also, on holding a newly established Health Services Executive (HSE) accountable for its performance
- Establish a HSE to manage the health services as "a single national entity"
- The HSE, it is proposed, is to comprise of:
    - A National Hospitals Office
    - A Primary Care, Community and Continuing Care Directorate
    - A National Shared Services Centre
- Abolish existing Health Boards and Health Authority structures. All remaining Boards (including the HSE) will be subject to audit against a new governance framework. The aim of the framework will be to ensure that boards operate within consistent parameters, designed to be accountable to deliver Value for Money (VFM)
- Strengthen and modernise supporting powers – the "plumbing of the system", as it were – such as Service Plans and Management Reports.

---

[2]   These included the Prospectus Report, *Audit of Structures and Functions in the Health System*, the *Report of the National Taskforce on Medical Staffing* (the Hanly Report), and the *Report of the Commission on Financial Management and Control Systems in the Health Service* (the Brennan Report).

[3]   For an excellent summary of the Health Reform Programme – as well as a critique of its proposals – see Minister for Health and Children's Statement to Dáil Eireann on 27 June 2003. See also *Dáil Debates*, 24 June 2003 and 19 June 2003, as well as the website of the DoHC.

The Programme deals with a number of issues that have long needed to be addressed. These include, in particular, the excessive fragmentation arising from a multiplicity (well over 50) of agencies and boards, which diffuse and blunt the transmission of policy and also entail administrative, management and IT costs arising from overlapping and duplication.

At the heart of the proposed new arrangements is the separation of the executive and non-executive functions of the DoHC. On the face of it, this represents a significant initiative – a major policy shift. The issue here centres on control, centralisation and the policy "mind-set": autonomy *versus* devolution. Under the proposed arrangements, executive functions are to be transferred to the HSE, which is to be overseen by, and accountable to, the DoHC.

Much, of course, depends on the flesh that is put on the bones of the HSE, in terms of its corporate structure and the extent of its autonomy. However, it is not immediately apparent that it represents a form of devolution that will encourage real innovation and enhanced patient outcomes at the *level of the hospital*, which is the point of service delivery. Effectively, power remains at the centre, albeit through a new administrative structure and a new set of reporting arrangements. In this regard, it is worth making the point that, in the major public hospitals, there is a robust platform for *using* greater autonomy. The development of Clinical Directorates, Clinicians in Management initiatives, strengthened financial and MIS systems all provide powerful arguments for an *empowering*, rather than *controlling*, ethos at the level of the Hospital.

There is also a compelling case for moving to multi-annual budgeting to support multi-annual Service Planning. Under existing arrangements, the annual Service Plan has become an administrative monster. The single year focus absorbs time and managerial resources while impeding the hospital/service provider, the Health Board – and the Department – from taking a strategic *multi-annual* perspective. Even the very best MIS and governance structures cannot operate effectively within a high pressure, spreadsheet-driven, 42-day planning cycle. It eliminates flexibility and subverts medium-term planning.

1.3 MEDICAL MANPOWER

The second strand of the Health Reform Programme deals, *inter alia*, with the need for managing effectively a reduction in the working hours for non-consultant hospital doctors (NCHDs) and concurrently, the development of Consultant-delivered services in the Acute/A&E sector. A proposed fundamental realignment of the delivery of A&E services in designated National Centres of Excellence, supported by a network of regional hospitals, is advocated. Woven through these proposals are the issues of education and training. In his Foreword to the Report, the Minister highlights two key points:

"Many of our hospitals are heavily dependent on non-consultant hospital doctors who work for lengthy periods without sufficient rest. This is not satisfactory either for the patient or for the doctors themselves. The EU European Working Time Directive will bring important changes to the working patterns of NCHD's from 1 August 2004 ... together with the case for a Consultant-provided service and the need for changes to medical education and training, [these developments] have significant consequences for the organisation of Acute Services."[4]

These are all key themes dealt with in successive chapters of this book, which spell out, *inter alia*, the compelling need for change, the impact that deficiencies in these areas are having on A&E and the systemic effects on the wider acute service.

The rationale for this is well illustrated in, for example, Beaumont – one of Dublin's largest acute hospitals. Consultant Dr David Hickey, in his chapter, points out that some 70% of admissions are emergencies, either direct transfers from regional hospitals or admissions through A&E. Frequently, the hospital operates at over 100% capacity – creating "trolley wards". It follows that more effective screening in A&E, as well as better consultant-delivered management of admissions and discharges, would shift the system away from its present over-dependence on frequently-stressed trainees, working excessive hours and engaged in the provision of "defensive" care, contributing to a "vicious circle" of over-crowded A&E Departments – serious congestion in the arteries of the system.

One immediate catalyst for change is, as noted, the prospective introduction of the European *Directive on Working Time*, requiring a reduction in working hours for NCHDs. In this regard, the Hanly Report proposes a phased reduction in the hours worked by junior doctors, from an *average* of 75 to a 48-hour week by 2009. Crucially, the report proposes the need – long proposed by the IHSA (see **Chapter VIII**) – for a more than doubling of the number of consultants: from some 1,731 to 3,600 on a phased basis, in order to provide a Consultant-delivered service within A&E.

More generally, when introducing the Health Reform Programme, the Minister stated:

"On acute hospitals, the reforms [will] clear the way for a reorientation of the hospital sector around national priorities ... and better value for money, underpinning the commitments made in the Health Strategy (2001). *It will provide a unitary approach to the delivery of hospital services and support the even and consistent introduction of consultant-delivered services in Ireland."*[5]

---

[4]   The Hanly Report, p.9.
[5]   Source: *Dáil Debates*, 24 June 2003.

The Hanly Report proposes the designation of a limited number of major hospitals, that have the facilities, volume of activities and expertise to provide the best possible service to patients. It is envisaged that they will be located in centres of population of some 350,000 or more. The economics are simple and compelling.

A population of roughly this size is needed to make such centres of excellence cost-effective *for the country as a whole* by ensuring the throughput of a "critical mass" of patients to justify a service delivered by teams of Consultants in the necessary specialisms: in practice, upwards of 50 consultants on call to deal with complex emergency cases.

These will, it is proposed, be supported by an integrated *regional* network of hospitals providing a wide range of medical and surgical procedures – augmented, where necessary, by additional specialists – and continuing to deal with 60 to 70% of total A&E cases.

Detailed recommendations are made in the Report regarding the organisation of acute hospital services in the ERHA and in the mid-western health boards, which will yield valuable experience for rolling -out a proposed phase II of the initiative.

In setting out the new configuration of acute hospitals services, the chairman of the Task Force, David Hanly, was at pains to point out that:

> *"the Government will not close any hospital nor does the Task Force recommend the closure of any hospital."*[6]

This may be intended to obviate the need to take highly-sensitive political decisions. But it hardly sense, in what has always been a highly-politicised process of hospital location, development and retention.

Whether, or not, the political commitment to rationalise the acute system is actually there is a moot point. Constituency politics in Ireland has sometimes taken precedence over the need to plan rationally in the wider national interest. It is – as, for example, France has shown – possible to break out of this unsustainable politically-driven cycle – but only if there is a corresponding degree of political courage. Otherwise, even the most rational change process may continue to be blocked by a "rationalise but not in my backyard" mentality. The French example shows that, once local political leadership understands the logic of change, and educates their constituencies regarding the benefits of structural change, it is possible to generate virtuous circle of structural reform.

A commitment *not* to close any hospital (this does not exclude new models of group GP clinics for small operations) immediately "front-loads" the investment requirements for implementing reform. This is, as noted, an issue of

---

[6]   *The Sunday Business Post*, 19 October 2003. This provides a succinct and accessible account of the substance of the Report by its Chairman. See also website of the DoHC. However, the Report merits a reading in its entirety.

enormous social and political sensitivity. Nonetheless, given the logic of concentrating resources and Value for Money – which are, after all, at the heart of the Government's *own* thinking – hard questions have to be asked. What is the rationale for the manner in which hospitals have developed in Ireland? Is there one? Is an open-ended commitment to keep *all* hospitals open, and even enhanced, consistent with the idea of developing cost-effective national centres of excellence? Is such an approach financially viable from the Exchequer's perspective and does it represent the best use of (increasing) scarce resources?

1.4 THE HANLY REPORT & REFORM

The Hanly Report, as the second strand of the Government's Health Reform Programme, raises three important issues that must be addressed.

The first involves *negotiations* with representative groups. In the past, there has been an undercurrent of uninformed criticism of Consultants, as if somehow they were part of the problem, instead of the key to the solution of A&E and acute care in Ireland. Consensus – building on how best to deliver and fund a consultant-delivered acute service – will require non-adversarial "high trust" negotiations, recognising, the rationale for, and the benefits of, Ireland's "public / private" mix.

A second issue involves *capacity*. It is important to point out, at the outset, that any acute service, including A&E, will work more efficiently if it is "backstopped" by investment in primary care. There are a number of new "models" based in part, on "Group Practice", which could form a "third-tier", supporting major acute hospitals, and regional/local hospitals.

The more immediate issue relates to consultant capacity. First, there is the length of time taken to process the projected number (see **Chapter XI**, Professor Brian Keogh) through specialist training. The second issue is the provision of the necessary support. Governments *always* underestimate the costs of filling Consultant posts. It is counter-productive to make such appointments *without also* factoring in the costs of nursing, administrative, technical and research support. In the reform process that is now envisaged – including the changes in medical manpower – it is absolutely imperative that priority be given to greatly-enhanced funding for medical research. This is not an optional extra – it goes to the very heart of building an adequate "research-driven knowledge infrastructure", around which to develop the new reforms.

Equally, provision must be made for *additional* physical capacity – including operating theatres and enhanced diagnostics in A&E and properly-serviced acute beds. At the margin, the existing system is operating above capacity. This generates clinical and operational risk.

A third issue relates to *funding*. The government set out costings at the time of the publication of the Health Strategy (2001). These are now obsolete. The fiscal environment has changed radically since 2001. And there are no detailed costings published by Government as part of the implementation of the "Health Reform Programme".

The front-loaded costs of the institutional reforms outlined above are significant. Equally, it is difficult to see the ultimate costs of the Hanly report – which is at the very heart of the reform programme in terms of patient care – being less than an *additional* €500 million plus (in current prices), when finally implemented. Even this is almost certainly conservative, since proposals, on the one hand, to develop consultant–delivered centres of excellences and, on the other hand, to retain (and augment, where necessary) *all* existing hospitals, amount to virtually an open-ended commitment:

It must be remembered, that these are additional to a cost-dynamic *already* built into the reform process. There are, for example, significant additional costs going forward, associated with the expansion of employment by some 25,000 between 1997 and 2001. There are also costs associated with the necessary upgrading/replacement of capital equipment in public hospitals, to say nothing of refurbishment/replacement of buildings (see **Chapter XV**, Dr David Hickey).

On any reasonable set of fiscal assumptions, the Exchequer resources to support the reform process are simply not there. In effect, the reform programme is wholly out of alignment with a sustainable set of Exchequer resources available for health: This raises the more fundamental issue of what tax rate(s) would be necessary to sustain existing, let alone greatly enhanced, acute facilities, over the medium-term. Health now absorbs a much greater proportion of tax revenue than in the middle 1990s. And the opportunity-cost of increasing health expenditure is increasing.

The key to "squaring this seemingly impossible circle" is to shift a greater proportion of expenditure – and risk – from the public sector balance sheet to the private sector. This will require not just a shift in policy but a change in mind-set. The PMI/self-funded sector is being – and has been for years – suffocated of investment, largely by Ireland's quasi-protectionist regulatory system – at the heart of which is Risk Equalisation, which is, almost certainly, contrary to the EU Treaty.[7]

Lip service is paid to an enlarged role for the private sector, for example, by arguing that the National Treatment Purchase Fund buys capacity from private hospitals. The reality is that it is becoming increasingly difficult for private hospital to remunerate capital. The paradox is, of course, that it is precisely

---

[7]   On this difficult – but extraordinary important issue – see the websites of BUPA Ireland, the Health Insurance Authority (HIA), the VHI as well as R Kinsella, *Private Health Insurance and the ineligibility of a RES under the EU Third Non Life Directive*, Centre for Insurance Studies, November 2003, *The Private Medical Insurance Market: Reform, Opportunities and Challenges* (with J O'Mahony), Centre for Insurance Studies, August 2000 and *Risk Equalisation, the Health Insurance Amendment Bill 2000 and the Irish PMI Market* (with A.J. Cully), *Financial Services Law Journal*, Vol. No.3 November 2001.

deregulation, competition and supply-side reform that has provided the dynamic to generate Exchequer resources – including health – *in the first place.*

What can be inferred from this is that if the twin-stranded reform proposals which provide the backdrop to this book are to work, there is an urgent need to incentivise – rather than stymie – competition and private sector development in acute healthcare: development that can *leverage* publicly-funded capacity, in the interests of greater equality of access and a more cost-effective acute system.

PART II: KEY ISSUES

Acute healthcare is a mosaic of interrelated processes, systems and protocols encompassing, for example, medical manpower, education and training, and capacity management as well as an appropriate mix between public and private funding and delivery of care. The contributions are, for the most part, treated under a major heading but it must be emphasised that, both in substance and scope, many of them speak to a number of themes.

II.I CUTBACKS

A first major theme relates to the extent and impact of "cutbacks" in the acute services, *post* the doubling of Exchequer expenditure between 1997 and 2001. In **Chapter I**, the Secretary-General of the DoHE provides a progress report on the National Health Strategy.

In this regard, he summarises the strategic model underlying the strategy:

> *"There has been an increase in activity in the Acute Hospital System, including the 'remarkable' growth in day procedures as well as the high – by OECD standards – occupancy rates".*

More generally, he characterises the system as a "very productive, very busy and, in relative terms, very efficient hospital system".

From a clinician's perspective, leading consultant David Hickey provides a devastating critique of the strains that are evident in the public hospital system – their underlying causes and the effects on both patients and staff. Dr Colm Quigley, President of the Irish Hospital Consultants Association (IHCA), highlights the impact of the cuts in consultant capacity on the provision of acute services – an issue which is central to the report of the National Task Force on Medical Staffing (the Hanly Report). Dr Quigley underlines – as do others – the implications for reform of the length of time it takes to "process" a prototypical consultant through the system.

The present shortage of consultant posts – and the systemic impact this has on the wider system – reflects, as Dr. Quigley notes, previous rounds of "cutbacks". There is another dimension to this, which is thrown into sharp relief by the increased emphasis on Value for Money (VFM). That is the attrition rate within medicine as a whole and, also, within specialisms, notably, general practice. Dr Richard Brennan, Chairman of the Irish College of GPs, points out that, "of the 75 GPs we train each year, we only retain two thirds in general practice, only half in full-time general practice". Dr Ruth Dowling who, having served her internship, took a principled decision to leave medicine altogether provides a personal – and compelling – case study of just *why* it is that the attrition rate is unacceptable. This subverts the efficiency of the system, and the concept of VFM invested in training. Dr Dowling's personal perspectives – notably, that because of the conditions which exist in regard to junior doctors, success and satisfaction for delivery patient care recur *in spite of*, rather than because of, "the system" – resonate certain of the points made by David Hickey and the more general argument for change in medical manpower as central to reform.

Quality of Care

A centrally important dimension of service delivery relates to the quality of healthcare. Hilary Coates provides an evaluation of the perspectives of different stakeholders of quality. Having reviewed empirical evidence on the issue, she rules out any clear-cut answer to the question of whether there is a "quality crisis" in healthcare.

However, she notes that there is increasing scepticism on the part of service-providers, leading to patient and client dissatisfaction, because staff feel even less valued.

> *"People and quality process make for a quality health service. A poor quality health service results from a poorly-designed and badly-operated process"*

Knowledge Management and "Cut Backs"

In a powerful and wide-ranging critique of "The Impact of Cutbacks and Expenditure Adjustment", Denis Doherty, Chief Executive of the Association of Health Boards highlights the issue of quality and the key role of "people centredness". He underlines the importance of a "knowledge workforce" to the development of a world-class health service:

> *"It is not possible to increase rapidly the size of a knowledge workforce. It is very unfair to a knowledge workforce to downsize it quickly because of a downturn in the economy".*

In the context of the present administration/medical "mix" skill shortage, he argues:

> *"When the health services are the designated battleground in political contexts, I think it is important that some regard be had to the potential negative impact that [uninformed criticism] can have on those who deliver an essential service".*

Education, Training & CPD

A closely related issue relates to the central role of education and training. It bears directly on the issue of capacity as well as quality. Professor Kevin

O'Malley, Chief Executive of the RCSI, addresses – head on – the over-dependence on overseas graduates, as well as the issue of appropriate structures for a sustainable post-graduate system that will facilitate the "processing" of the specialists required to support the system. Professor Brian Keogh – a past president of the Royal College of Physicians – provides an detailed overview of the framework of training programmes, in terms of structures and procedures. He highlights the progress with the DoHE in developing appropriate structures to be embedded in specialist training process. This is vitally important, since it is on the basis of this cooperation that progress with future initiatives, including those in the Hanly Report, must be built. Importantly, Professor Keogh highlights deficiencies in the supply of certain specialists, as well as the need to align the numbers coming into specialist training programmes to the available capacity.

On the more general issue of education, Tony McNamara, Chief Executive of Cork University Hospital, highlights the *ad hocery* in the funding of university teaching hospitals and a rigorous analysis of just why they are grossly underfunded, for their input into the health system, including acute care. The inadequate scale of funding has been more or less successfully ignored by policy-makers. The reform process underlines the need for greater transparency, and related reforms, in this absolutely key area.

Primary/Acute Sector Management
The importance of the interface between the primary and acute sectors is one of the key policy – and practice – insights in recent years. A&E Departments that are clinically effective (which means more and better diagnostics as well as Consultant-provided services) are demonstrably more cost-effective arteries into the acute system, compared with the existing over-stretched, under-resourced departments. Equally, GPs play a crucial role as "gatekeepers" into the acute system. Dr Michael Boland, Dean of Post Graduate Studies at the Irish College of GPs reiterates a point made by Dr. Richard Brennan, namely, that pressure on the acute sector is highly sensitive to the referral rate by GPs.

This underlines the importance of investment in this area, even in an environment of cutbacks. The solution to the structural problems in healthcare is not, Dr Boland argues, to be found solely in an acute sector with more specialists but in a better balance between "generalist" GPs (which will require additional investment) and acute specialists.

Demand Management
In a fiscal environment where "cutbacks" are the order of the day, there are two possible responses. These are not mutually exclusive, but it is useful all the same to differentiate between the two approaches. The first is to operate on the supply-side through, for example, deregulation, competition and incentives. We return to this shortly.

A key issue in this regard is that the increase in demand, and in expenditure, does not appear to be systematically related to epidemiological developments – they are not driven by major shifts in mortality or morbidity. Dr Boland evaluates possible ways to moderate demand within, importantly, an ethical and humane system. In this context, he argues that the system that currently operates in the acute hospital system:

"... needs to be abolished [and] ... replaced by a system where you have providers of healthcare capacity in an open market and where access is there for patients of all catagories ... a single service with doctors on a single site with choice for all ... it is possible, within that context, not overnight but eventually as a matter of strategic policy to have multiple payers using mixed methods of payment".

II.2 "CHANGE DRIVERS"

An absolutely fundamental driver of change in the demand for acute care is the changing demographics, evident in the CSO Census of Population. Aidan Punch, Senior Statistican with the Central Statistics Office (CSO), points out that we have been experiencing very high rates of growth in our population:

"far in excess of anything experienced in other EU or OECD countries ... We are also living in a golden age in terms of dependency ratios. It is going to get worse from here on in".

This implies that the opportunity-cost of expenditure on health is going to increase.

Punch makes two other important points in terms of policy. The first relates to the robust projections for continued rapid growth in population along the eastern seaboard. This has implications for continued pressure on already over-stretched acute facilities in the ERHA.

The second merits more than a passing reference. The numbers of those over 65 is set to double by 2030, while those over 80 will more than double. The implications of this CSO projection for strategic planning in the acute sector have been incisively evaluated by Dr. Mary Codds:

"We currently have around 11% of the population aged 65 and over. They comprise of about one quarter of all in-patients in the acute hospital system. Even more significantly, they occupy 45% of all beds in the acute hospitals.....of course, there is a certain amount of inappropriate placement ... but if we look at the UK or the rest of Europe, the over 65 population is about 15% -16% of the population, and they occupy if all acute hospital beds"...

what this means is that:

"We are looking at a huge need for acute services, which need to be supplemented by home-care services, rehabilitation, convalescence and long-term care ... acute hospital

bed capacity ... is just one part of [the problem] no matter what we put in now, we need to keep thinking in terms of re-engineering these services – even if its acute capacity now that can be re-engineered in time. We simply need more capacity in the system[8]

II.3 COMPETITION & INCENTIVISING PRIVATE CAPACITY

The question of capacity is highlighted, amongst others, by David Hickey and, also, Denis Doherty. Capacity encompasses not only properly-serviced acute beds, theatre capacity and medical manpower, but also the infrastructure, for example, step-down facilitites for elderly acute patients, which can leverage new investment in acute capacity. It is clear from Punch's analysis of CSO data that the capacity issue will not go away. Equally, the already obvious scaling back – in the form of "cutbacks", "mothballing" and recruitment embargos, as well as the deferral of commissioning beds – of increases in capacity projected in the Health Strategy (2001) points to real difficulties for Government in providing the *additional* capacity, not alone in A&E, but in acute facilities in regional hospitals, that is an integral part of the Health Reform Programme. There is, quite simply, a contradiction: cutbacks in the Health Strategy November 2001 proposals coexisting with proposals for major investment in Health Reform Programme (2003). There is, of course, additional capacity that can be generated through the initiatives outlined by the Secretary-General of the DoHE and, more generally, by VFM. But there is a limit to this and potential gains dwarf actual requirements. Capacity rates close to – and, in some instances, in excess of 100% – are untenable and generates risks for patients.

The Government's programme is focussed almost wholly on enhancing public capacity. It has, effectively, dabbled with private sector capacity through, for example, the Special Purchase Treatment Fund. And while there are fiscal incentives to increase investment in private hospitals, the impact of these is effectively stymied.

In an in-depth and authoritative case study, Mark Moran, Chief Executive of the Mater Private Hospital, demonstrates how the private sector has been at the leading-edge of innovation in the acute sector, while at the same time being effectively hamstrung by the difficulty of remunerating capital, *at a time of excess demand*. A number of private hospitals have closed – there has been a single major initiative in the form of a new acute hospital in Galway. Capacity is needed to make good existing deficiencies, to meet increased demand and to plan for the future. A key point made by Moran in this regard is that the present PMI market is effectively a "claims-settlement" system rather than an example of a competitive market, which is what is needed.

---

[8]   Dr. Mary Codds, speaking at the Seventh Annual PMI conference, *Acute Healthcare in Ireland: Cutbacks, Change and Challenges*, Centre for Insurance Studies, Smurfit Graduate School, Dublin, November, 2002.

PART III

III.I   CHALLENGES

This takes us to the issue of funding and the role of competition and market-based funding. In a rigorous overview of Ireland's growth prospects and the implications for public spending (including healthcare), Robbie Kelleher makes a number of centrally important points. First, Ireland has now moved into a "world of low numbers", including a greatly reduced scope for public spending. Second, the doubling of public spending on health between 1997 and 2001 has not produced anything like a corresponding increase in outcomes. Third, Ireland is going to have to get used to a "new normality": one in which "cutbacks" mean precisely that, rather than increases that are out of line with what the Exchequer can afford, by orders of magnitude. This will impose on politicians the necessity of making difficult funding decisions on health, as well as on other large spending departments.

Kinsella argues that the highly socially-regressive effects of a lack of capacity in the acute system can *only* be addressed by allowing competition in the self-funded (including PMI) sector as well as by a focus on the supply-side, including deregulation. In the absence of a reform of the supply-side, proposals in the Health Reform Programme (however well-founded) will be aspirational. The lack of competition in PMI – created by regulatory barriers and a failure to comply with the EU Single Market – is simultaneously generating "market failure" in Long-Term Care insurance, the importance of which has been highlighted by Punch and others.

In this regard, an absolutely central set of contributions is the debate between Professor Alistair Woods, Chairman of the Health Insurance Authority (HIA) and Aidan Cassells, Deputy Chief Executive of AXA and Chairman of the EU Single Market *Comité Européen des Assurances*. Professor Woods provides a systematic analysis of the nature and operation of the Risk Equalisation Scheme (RES), which is at the heart of PMI regulatory regime. Cassells sets out the perspective of a major European insurer who, having evaluated the scope for offering PMI products in Ireland, concluded that the regulatory regime was a major barrier to entry and, almost certainly, contrary to the Treaty and unjustified under the terms of the EU Third Non-Life Directive. He points out, in particular, that "he has never believed that an RES could be justified under Article 54 – the general good provisions" – upon which the government developed its case for an RES-supply because the private system was not a genuine "alternative" to the Public Acute System. What all of this means is that an overstretched public system, in urgent need of being supplemented by private capacity, is being subverted by a failure to deregulate along the lines of other sectors and, also, by deficiencies in the governance of the PMI market. The consequences are inequality of access and a major impediment to the development of a new model of acute care based on the *total* capacity of the private and public sectors.

Reforming the PMI Market and Supply – Side Investment

Government will have to revisit the whole issue of the reform of the private health insurance (PHI) market. This will become progressively more urgent as the public acute system comes under increasing strain and the fiscal difficulties of Exchequer-only funding of reforms (the present policy) become more apparent.

The reality is that the key reforms set out in the White Paper on PHI (1999[9]) have either failed or have not been implemented. The Health Insurance (Amendment) Act, 2001 – at the heart of which is a Risk Equalisation Scheme (RES) – has determined market entry, impeded competition and subverted the EU Internal Market. A mechanism – introduced in 1996, and legislated for in 2001, has proved to be untenable – at a huge cost in terms of deterring investment by potential entrants into the PHI and, equally important, the Long Term Care insurance market.

The Government remains the owner of the dominant insurer in the market, the ultimate regulator of the market as well as effectively determining the stock of bed stock as well as retaining control over PHI premia. These circumstances are wholly contrary to the principles of good governance, which is a major theme running through the Health Reform Programme, as well as related reports.

PHI premia will *have* to continue to rise over the medium-term. If this increase is to be kept to a minimum, there will have to be real competition in the PHI market – as well as wider supply-side reforms. Competition is the most effective antidote to that most insidious threat to the sustainability of the acute system. The problem is simple: competition which should have been central to the 1999-2001 reforms (as it has been across all other sectors of the economy) has been "crowded-out" of reform of the PHI market.

The net effect has been that the capacity generated by the private sector has been kept artificially low which, in turn, has restricted the *total* capacity of the system available for *all* patients. Capacity and innovation should be driven by the needs and preferences of patients, leaving the market to contribute in a meaningful way to equitable, efficient and cost-effective models of patient care. A *fundamental* reform of a near-suffocated PHI system will mean just that: nothing – including community rating – can be taken as a given, in the search for greater equity, social solidarity and affordability – a greater contribution to capacity from the PHI/Long-Term Care insurance markets.

---

[9]   *White Paper on PHI Reform*, Dublin Department of Health and Children, 1999.

III.2. NEED FOR DEREGULATION IN THE PUBLIC, AS WELL AS PRIVATE, SYSTEMS

The whole issue of the lack of innovation and deregulation is further extended in an important critique by Professor Muiris Fitzgerald, Dean of UCD Medical School. He makes a compelling case for deregulation *not alone* within the private sector but, more importantly, within the public system. This is an important contribution to the whole debate on reform in acute care and the scope for action that lies directly within the Government's direction.

A key element in developing a new and depoliticised acute healthcare system rests with medical service-providers themselves. There has never been an integrated, physician-driven, vision of what is needed and what is achievable. Instead, within an essentially "top-down" process, the initiative has rested with politicians and policy-drivers, informed by albeit successive reports. Medical service-providers have responded on a unilateral and reactive basis to Government-announced reforms and strategies.

The point is that the medical service-providers themselves – Consultants, doctors (including importantly, GPs), nurses and other specialists represented by different representative colleges – have never challenged the policy-making *status quo* by generating their own integrated strategic healthcare plan, setting out goals, policy instruments and structures as well as anticipated patient outcomes – and the funding implications.

This would provide a "benchmark" against which to evaluate the present policy-making process: a benchmark that was informed by medical service-providers who, after all, have front-line knowledge not alone of the issues, gaps and problems but equally, of "Best Practice" in terms of new clinical and therapeutic praises, including the necessary "enabling" IT. This would ensure that policy was not alone informed, but had the necessary "buy-in" from the different healthcare constituencies, to give a "fair wind" to change.

More broadly, what is clearly needed is a new form of "Partnership" reform process, including an integrated input from medical service-providers, on the lines sketched out above. Such an approach stands a better chance of addressing, within a realistic timescale (including election horizons), three interrelated and seemingly-intractable issues:

- The inexorable rise in public expenditure on health, which does not reflect epidemiological evidence that people as a whole are more sick or more in need of acute services

- The inequalities, inequities and lack of an ethical base on which reform can be built

- The "Healthcare Productivity Conundrum" (see **Chapter XIV**).

This can be expressed briefly as follows. There has, on the one hand, been an unprecedented increase in aggregate as well as sectoral (for example, cardiovascular) expenditures on health. Between 1997 and 2002/3, Exchequer expenditure on health rose from €3.6 billion to €9.3 billion – corresponding to a rise in the percentage of <u>total</u> government spending from 19% to 24%. For some measures – for example, healthcare expenditure as a percentage of GDP – international comparisons can be seriously misleading. What *can* be said is that the increase, in terms in the opportunity-cost, with regard to "crowding-out" of other policy options, is rising. A simple example illustrates this point. In 1997, healthcare expenditure absorbed over 50% of total income tax receipts – this has now risen to some 100%.[10] [11]

Equally, on the other hand, there has been nothing like a corresponding increase in outcomes, throughput and activity rates have, as the Minister and the Department of Health and Children, increased. But not to the same extent. The evidence, at the margin, is indicative of increasing strain on the acute system as well as rationing in the form of "cutbacks" of various kinds, including the *de facto* decommissioning of significant number of acute beds. We are now, paradoxically, in the position of facing into prospective reforms at the most fundamental level: but reforms that have no published costings and – as indicated above – which the Exchequer simply cannot fund, going forward.

III.3. CHALLENGES

The reality of a strong ethical dimension to the reform of the acute system needs to be addressed. This encompasses a number of dimensions: that is, inequality in terms of access based on medical need; the societal effects of anti-social behaviour and of social deprivation and, third, specific ethical challenges newly emergent in acute health care. It is widely acknowledged that the existing system is unfair and inequitable, denying timely access to parts of the population. "Trolley wards" and overcrowded A&E departments are symptomatic of this. Dr Michael Boland argues that "we need to talk a great deal about ethics as we get into the reform process". Equally, Dr. Richard Brennan argues that "there are ethical issues we must ask about where we are going as a society" and he provides graphic evidence of the lack of care in society as a result of an erosion of key social values, including the abandonment of elderly relatives in casualty departments. It is difficult to argue with his view that "poverty and depravation are really the key markers for health outcomes in the country".

There are profound inequalities in the Irish healthcare system, including acute care and the A&E system. The Government's Chief Medical Officer (CMO), Dr James Kiely, in the first *Annual Report of the Chief Medical Officer* (1999) highlighted the pervasiveness and magnitude of occupational class health

---

[10]   Minister for Finance at the launch of the Government's Health Reform Programme, 19 June 2003.

[11]   See critique by Dr Muiris Houston of an evaluation of ERHA data by the Irish Patients Association, *Irish Times*, 10 May 2003.

inequalities. Significantly, the report *Inequalities in Health in Irelan*
published by the Department of Community Health and General
was published at the same time (2001) as the Government's He:
which committed itself unequivocally to a more equitable system,
based on need. The TCD analysis showed, in stark terms, just how great is the
divide in Ireland in terms of health status, health outcomes and access to
healthcare.[12] The inequitable – and unethical – features of the system include
waiting list management.[13]

In a powerfully-argued analysis of health behavioural trends among young
people, the Secretary-General of the DoHC points out that "when we look at
the European *versus* Irish experience around consumption of alcohol and drugs,
there is a serious cause for concern". He goes on to point out that, because of
these trends, we need to redouble our efforts at every level. We can infer an
important policy implication from this and related contributions in the book.
The effects of behavioural trends in regard to alcohol (and the related effects on
road traffic accidents in A&E and in the wider acute and rehabilitative sector)
and drugs among young people will feed through successive age cohorts:
exacerbating outcomes arising from other factors, they will reinforce pressure
on the acute system. And in pretty well the same time horizon when the impact
of aging on the acute sector will be most evident.

Denis Doherty, in his chapter, asks the key ethical question: are we investing
in healthcare for a *social* – or for a *purely financial* – return? At a macro level,
David Hickey reiterates the point that our medical staffing practices have been
based on the highly unethical practice of "stealing" the healthcare trainees, on
which developing countries depend.

It will be evident that the issue of ethics goes a great deal deeper than an
enunciation of the principles of fairness, equality of access and so on.

The articulation of ethics into healthcare – especially acute healthcare – is
particularly important in an environment of "cutbacks" and change in policy
regime. Ethics also embraces whole new sets of issues with which
representative bodies in the Medical Council, representative colleges and
individual hospitals are already grappling. Ireland, to its credit, has engaged in
passionate debate about the objective nature of the right to life. Soon – indeed
already – the ethical debate is moving to a genome-related clinical and research
applications platform. Philosophy is now an integral part of the reform process.
The absence of clearly-articulated objective values – both social and, more
especially moral – will create a vacuum at the heart of any fundamental reform
process.

---

[12] For an insightful and informed analysis of the Health Reform Programme (2003), see O'Farrell,
F.: *Equity and Access in Healthcare: urgent case for diagnosis and treatment*, mimeo, the Adelaide Hospital
Society. See also Wren, Maev-Ann: *Unhealthy State*.

[13] See Kinsella, R.: Waiting List: Analysis and Evaluation, *Journal of Irish Management (IBAR)*,
December 2003.

The purpose of the expert and diverse contributions to this book – which add up to a positive, constructive and holistic critique – is to shed light on these and related issues – in a word, to inform the debate initiated by the publication of the Health Reform Programme (2003).

For the first time, leading health correspondents attended, and actively participated in, the PMI conference. They provided a valuable, but unreported, input to the discussion. Nonetheless, their participation is reflected in the themes and successive chapters in this book.

II

THE NATIONAL HEALTHCARE STRATEGY: A PROGRESS REPORT ON INITIATIVES IN THE ACUTE SECTOR

MICHAEL KELLY

SECRETARY-GENERAL, DEPARTMENT OF HEALTH & CHILDREN

First, while the title of my paper could be taken to refer to the acute hospital system, my own definition of the acute sector is wider. I think you can only meaningfully discuss the acute sector in a context where you are also talking about the other pieces of the healthcare system that connect up with the acute hospitals. So, whether we are talking about a needs basis, a strategy or planning discussion, a resource-based discussion or whatever, it is important to look at the whole of the acute system in this wider context.

HEALTH STRATEGY

This strategy is the framework through which we are developing agendas in acute care, non-acute services and elsewhere. It has four key principles –

- Equity
- People-centeredness
- Quality
- Accountability.

These lead us to an articulation of four national goals:

- Better health for everyone
- Fair access
- Appropriate and responsive care
- A high-performing health system.

FRAMEWORKS FOR CHANGE:

What we are working through at present are what we call six *Frameworks for Change*:

- Reforming the acute hospitals
- Strengthening primary care
- Funding of the system
- Organisational reform
- Developing human resources
- Developing information systems.

Although our discussion today is about the acute system, it will be obvious that there are inter-dependencies between this and developing human resources, funding issues, organisational reform, developing information or strengthening primary care. To the extent that we do or do not follow through on each of the other five headings, there will be an impact on what gets done in the acute system.

OVERVIEW OF MEDICAL TRENDS IN IRELAND & EU

Again, let's just remind ourselves what we are talking about - the business of achieving health and social gain. It's interesting to look at where we are starting from. In relation to whether it's the acute hospitals, the primary care system or continuing care, its useful to look at some of the basic health indicators – both as a baseline and also as a commentary on how we are doing in relation to other European countries.

Slide 1 presents a familiar message. In relation to death rates overall, and the other side of the coin – increasing life expectancy, the news is broadly good, if you look at the period from the early 1980s to the end of the 1990s. In particular, with heart disease, you can see a very significant decrease in the standardised mortality rate for those under 65 – over 50% for males, and almost 60% for females. So, in terms of impact, we can show positive health results at that broad level.

If you look at Slide 2, again the trend on heart disease from 1980 to 1999 is downward. However, in reference to our European peers, there is still a gap there. That, to me, says that we are moving in the right direction but we can do better. Similarly, in relation to strokes (Slide 3), when you look at the male and female death rates, the trend is in the right direction, with females coming out somewhat better. That is, as it were, the good news. But when you look at Ireland and the EU in relation to all cancers – again with regard to the mortality rate, the trend is in the right direction but there is that significant gap indicating an area of potential improvement.

SLIDE 1:

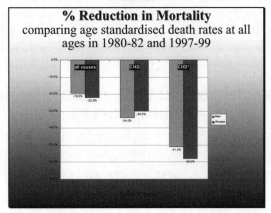

SLIDE 2:

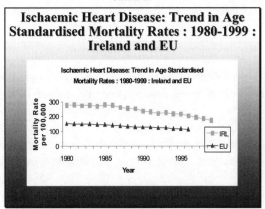

SLIDE 3:

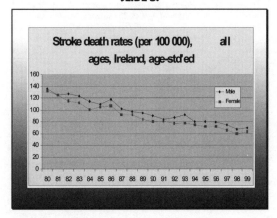

You could conclude, based on some of the general improvements in lifestyle – for example, reduced prevalence of smoking, in healthcare, in general economic and living conditions, in people's living standards, in people's education standards – that, with all that has happened since the beginning of that dataset in 1980, things are all pointing in the right direction.

HEALTH BEHAVIOURAL TRENDS AMONG YOUNG PEOPLE

But I think there is very sobering news in an analysis of health behaviours among young people. From the survey data available, the picture that emerges is of:

- Increasing prevalence of smoking among children and young people, particularly among young females

- Reduced inclination to exercise – once young people get into their teens and, again, particularly among young women

- Obesity – key issues around that are diet and exercise and, again when you look at exercise, there is a 'drop out' effect, particularly among young females.

One very significant feature here is the socio-economic gradient involved in both these health behaviours and subsequent health outcomes. Furthermore, when we look at the European vs. Irish experience around consumption of alcohol and drugs, there is serious cause for concern. In the very young teen years, there is a heavy consumption of alcohol, particularly relative to their ability to consume alcohol. Young people, at alarmingly early ages, resort to recreational drugs.

SLIDE 4:

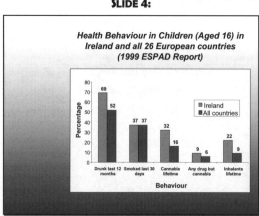

What does all of this say? In the normal course of events, because the ageing of our population is taking place at a different point in time relative to other European countries, we should be able to relax and plan ahead. Because of the health risk factors that we can now see in young people, it seems to me that we need to redouble our efforts at every level, starting with primary prevention and moving through primary, secondary and continuing care.

There is absolutely no reason, based on the demographic and health behaviour trends that are coming through, and what we can perceive in young people in particular, to slow down on anything we are currently doing. In fact, however hard we are running right now, we should be running a lot harder and be preparing to run even harder still - both in terms of prevention but also in terms of what we need to do to prepare, not just for the ageing of the population, but increasingly the problems that will emerge in the middle years for these age cohorts, as they come through. I hope I don't sound too alarmist about this, but it is a really serious problem reflecting broader societal concerns, as well as being a health problem.

This leads me to a key theme: How does our health system attempt to respond to the health problems and health issues coming through?

DEVELOPING STRATEGIC RESPONSES

You cannot look seriously at the needs of acute hospitals, without also looking at strengthening primary care and providing for people in need of continuing care – some of that at community level, but there is also a growing need for long-term non-acute care in residential settings. That is the outcome of the analysis we have done around acute hospital needs. In going for the addition to capacity that is reflected in the strategy commitment – 3,000 additional beds, I am conscious that this figure is part of a range that emerged from the analysis. Quite deliberately, the 3,000 figure has been picked, on the assumption that we are also going to strengthen the primary care system and the service capacity available to people in the community and in continuing care in institutional settings.

PRIMARY CARE

I want to start by talking about primary care. We should only think about dealing with work in acute hospitals that is appropriate to that setting. We know from international experience and research that primary care is the appropriate setting for 90% to 95% of health needs. Therefore, the need for acute hospital capacity should be thought of as a residual – to address what cannot be handled through a well-developed and properly functioning primary care system.

In the primary care strategy document, for those of you who have not had the opportunity to look at it, there is a diagram entitled *The Clinical Iceberg* which, I believe, demonstrates this very well. It's essentially a big iceberg that has a huge part of it covered by self-care, primary prevention and then we move into a smaller block where we are into primary care and then we move into an

even smaller block where we are into the acute hospital system. This puts the issue in context. While we need to get on with getting the acute system right, alongside that there is an equally important job to be done, given the state of development in relation to primary care, in developing the primary care system. That is why I am putting such emphasis on it.

The challenge here is to develop capacity for primary care, based on a 'team approach', where each member of the team contributes their competencies, skills and knowledge. It depends on viewing the needs of the consumer of healthcare in a holistic way and acknowledging that there are a number of inputs that go towards meeting the level of care that an individual person requires.

There is a huge challenge in this and we will talk about some of the issues that arise. In the short term, what we are trying to do is to ensure that out-of-hours cover provided through general practitioner co-ops, with the co-operation of general practitioners and Health Boards, are in place nationwide as quickly as possible. We are not at that stage yet, but hopefully we can move to that point as quickly as possible.

The basic constituents of the primary care model, which is the subject of the primary care strategy, are summarised on **Slide 5**. We are talking about a team, and on the right-hand side of the slide you can see the make-up of that team. The general practitioners are there obviously – and we have nurses, midwives, healthcare assistances, physiotherapists, occupational therapists, social workers and some administrative support.

SLIDE 5:

The idea is that these teams will serve populations of 3,000 to 7,000 people – responding to a very clearly articulated requirement in the consultation process around the strategy for access to well-organised, co-ordinated, quality services at community level. People did not talk about 'primary care' – but they did talk about those requirements in the form of the package that they would like to see delivered at community level.

We are talking then about these teams being linked to a wider network of practitioners. Again, the idea here is a highly-integrated operation, with lots of IT and communications support, based ultimately on an electronic patient record where there would be easy transfer of information relevant to each practitioner between members of the team and, ultimately, interaction with the acute hospitals as well. Clearly, there are issues around this in relation to confidentiality that need to be looked at and followed through.

Under the banner of the Task Force (the small executive team to drive implementation) and the Steering Committee (including all the stakeholders) and with a budget of €8m in 2002 and a repeat of that in 2003, we are now making some headway. The approach being taken is to drive the thinking through of the model on the basis of a set of pilot projects. The selection of the first 10 of those has just been put in place. We need to use them to think through all the practical issues that arise when working through this model. There are a lot of outstanding questions that still need to be worked through in a practical way through action research.

Obviously, ensuring the continuing commitment of stakeholders is important. We hope to do that through continuing dialogue with stakeholders – in a very intense way – both through the Steering Group and through the sort of conference we had in Galway recently, where we brought together 160 of the key stakeholders over two days and did a lot of intensive workshops around the practical issues. We need to put in place an evaluation framework that picks up the lessons, and creates the basis on which we can transplant those lessons to later generations of projects. Community involvement and how we organise that is another key question. Fully exploiting the potential of ICT is obviously very important, as is the creation of linkages between primary care and the acute hospital system.

ACUTE HOSPITAL SYSTEM

Against this backdrop, in terms of health indicators and the primary care level, what are we planning in relation to the acute hospitals?

First, I want to take a look at activity in the Irish acute hospital system. The acute hospitals are putting through 920,000 treatments *per annum* as we speak – and that workload is increasing year on year. In 2001, there was a 5% increase in that figure over the year 2000 – from the same bed stock. In 2002, again, there is a significant increase in activity coming through in the bottom line. In relation to daywork specifically, a significant component of the work that now goes on in acute hospitals – there is an increase of some 14% coming through in 2002.

This order of increase in day procedures is remarkable. In 1980 for example (admittedly over 20 years ago), that figure would have accounted for 2% of acute hospital activity. It is now close to 40% in 2001. Some of the Dublin teaching hospitals have exceeded the 50% benchmark at this stage.

What is it about? It is about a shorter length of stay. It is about moving people more quickly through the system. It is about availing of the newer technologies that allow many procedures, both investigative and treatment, to be done on a day basis.

What is this saying about our bed occupancy? We can look again at some international comparisons on this. Occupancy levels are very very high. In 2001, an overall occupancy of about 85% – in some hospitals, a bed occupancy rate that exceeds 100%.

I have spoken about the significant increase in day-case activity – the graph from 1980 to 2000 (**Slide 6**) shows it shooting skywards. This growth has derived from the level of need in the population, linked to improvements in treatments and technologies, and fuelled by a very hefty increase in investment – both capital and non-capital – in the system. While the advent of newer technologies generate their own demands to some extent, by and large this growth reflects a response by the hospitals to previously unmet need in the population.

SLIDE 6:

On length of stay, I have commented that one of the trends we are seeing is shortening length of stay. The graph in **Slide 7** shows Ireland's position among OECD countries. The data is from 1996, because that is the most recent data we have from the OECD – although our own more recent data would not show any disimprovement in the Irish position. So, on length of stay, we score very highly by international standards – we have a very short length of stay.

When you link the stay to a fixed bed stock, clearly you would expect the occupancy rate to be relatively high (**Slide 8**). Again, among OECD countries, Irish hospitals are the most busy in terms of occupancy.

SLIDE 7:

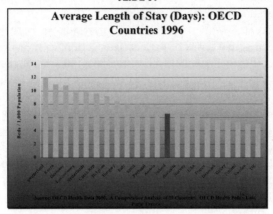

SLIDE 8:

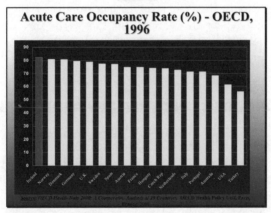

The picture suggested by the data is of a very productive, very busy and, in relative terms, very efficient hospital system. What do people who were treated in these hospitals say about their experience? I quote from the survey carried out in 2000 by the Irish Society for Quality in Healthcare, which tested the attitudes of 1,800 patients who had been through the acute system – they were not commentators on the side as it were. They were not people who hadn't yet reached the system, who would presumably have expressed stronger dissatisfaction. But it is significant that 96% were either 'satisfied' or 'very satisfied' with the level of quality of care they got from the system.

Now, that is not to say that they were perfectly happy with everything that had happened to them. I think the significant thing here is that overall satisfaction rates are very high, despite the busyness of the system we are talking about. In the course of the health strategy, we also did some work around this issue of patient or customer satisfaction. Again, it was professionally done and the results are reflected in the index scores of satisfaction with hospital-based services.

The main point I want to draw from the results of both surveys is the contrast between actual levels of patient satisfaction, as measured in a formal survey, and the on-going commentary on the hospital system, usually based on extrapolation from a particular experience at a point in time. The overall level of satisfaction with hospital services as recorded in this survey was 84%. This was a somewhat lower level of satisfaction than the earlier survey. The relative scores are interesting – for example, Accident & Emergency and Casualty departments scored relatively low. This is not surprising, given the busy places that A & E Departments are. On the Outpatient side, again I am not terribly surprised with the relatively low score, given that, as the strategy acknowledges, there is a need to strengthen considerably the infrastructure around Outpatient services.

What I would suggest is that the overall satisfaction ratings recorded, based on direct experience of the system, as distinct from the running commentary about it, does not reflect the state of constant crisis that one hears about regularly. I am not suggesting that this is the only outcome on which to judge performance but, in a patient-centred service, it must be a serious consideration.

PROGRESS ON OTHER KEY PRINCIPLES

I now want to look at the principles of Equity, People-Centeredness, Quality and Accountability in relation to the acute hospitals and to trace the aspects of the system we are trying to influence in response. Principally, we are talking about the aspects of the acute hospitals that relate to the public/private mix and addressing, in particular, the principle of Equity.

It is in the context of the mixed public/private campus we find in the public hospital system that the means by which we distribute the benefits of public investment across the population becomes critical. The Treatment Purchase Fund (TPF) represents a particular response to this whole equity concern.

In relation to People-centeredness, we are talking about things like access, including aspects such as location, timing, appointment systems and a reasonable response when things go wrong. People-centredness is also concerned with our approach to complaints and, overall, with providing a civilized response to people coming in through the door. It also entails mutual respect in our internal relationships, and implies a lot more attention to how we deal with health staff. I will deal with what we are doing on the Human Resource side of things later.

On the Quality principle, the emphasis will be on development of and adherence to standards and protocols. However, putting in place the additional capacity needed will also be a pre-requisite to ensuring the maintenance of high standards over the medium-term.

Accountability is about defining much more precisely the role we expect of individual hospitals within the system. It will also entail more transparent methods for funding, relying more heavily on case-mix, and a huge premium being placed on information, and its analysis.

A frequently asked question in relation to the hospital system is how do we drive Value for Money (VFM)? The primary instrument we rely on here is a heavier reliance on case-mix in determining the overall budgets of particular hospitals. Case-mix relates the average cost for the whole system for a particular treatment to a particular hospital. It is based on Irish costs and on diagnosis related groups, an internationally-accepted way of categorising treatments in hospitals. It is both objective and designed to drive best practices and the best outcomes in terms of cost through the system, by requiring hospitals to address the average Irish cost-per-case. At the moment, there is a blend in each hospital's budget that is made up from the base, built up through history, and an element that is case-mix-based. As we go forward, the blend will be strengthened in relation to case-mix. From the experience to date with this case-mix model, it is clear that it does in fact create an incentive towards efficiency in the system.

In relation to planning of additional capacity, the Government has accepted the need to plan for an additional 3,000 beds over the next decade. The analysis underpinning the need for 3,000 beds has addressed demographic projections, technological advances (in so far as we can), and the move towards day-work. It has also factored in pent-up demand as reflected in the waiting lists and takes account of age-specific utilisation rates. So it is an exercise that we stand over. I would make the point that the 3,000 additional beds represents a point along a range. It could have been somewhat higher – it might have been somewhat lower. Critically, it does assume development in the areas alongside the acute system as well.

We are already making progress on this commitment. We should ave 600 of the additional beds by end-December, with the balance of 109 in place early in the New Year. A deliberate decision has been made about the use of these beds: Given the imbalance in waiting time for public and private patients in the public system and the fact that the planned 80/20 mix in public hospitals had slipped to 71% public/29% private for elective work, there was a need to adjust the mix. Quite deliberately, we have adopted a policy position that the additional capacity going in will be for public patients. Hospital managers will be expected to manage the bed stock to reflect this policy position.

CAPACITY & THE ROLE OF THE PRIVATE SECTOR

Additions to capacity in the acute hospital system can come in a number of different ways. In the 2002 tranche, we are talking about publicly-funded and publicly-managed beds. On the other hand, as part of the strategy, there is a clear message about the complementarity of the public and private hospital systems. Alongside health developments, through the Finance Acts, a series of incentives is being offered to private investors to establish private hospital facilities.

There is evidence of considerable interest both domestically and internationally in this area, reflected in the number of enquiries coming in. This points to the need for a strategic relationship between the independent private hospital sector and the public system. The first instalment of this is in place through the Treatment Purchase Fund and through some of the contracting already underway with the public system – for example, contracting to buy services from the private sector to deal with waiting lists.

Through the Treatment Purchase Fund we see a more overt strategic relationship emerging. I think we can anticipate a further broadening of that relationship, provided there is a coincidence of interest between the public and private sectors. The nature of this strategic relationship needs to be worked out in more depth. Critical features will be concerned with standards of quality, price – clearly – and accountability.

All private institutions or service providers operate within a number of existing accountability frameworks – for example, professional accountability to their shareholders and perhaps to others. However, I believe there would be a demand, from a public interest point of view, for some degree of regulation in relation to the private system, if this strategic relationship is to develop to the point where a significant volume of demand on the public system was to be addressed through private hospitals.

On one other aspect of this partnership, we have been putting our toe in the water as regards Public/Private Partnerships (PPP) in planning for the development of Community Nursing Units for older people. We are talking about 850 new beds in the Eastern and Southern regions. It is a pilot project – if it works successfully, hopefully we will be able to go further with this model of provision.

On waiting lists, when we look at what is actually happening - not so much on waiting lists, but on waiting time for some of the key specialties – we are seeing significant progress. Admittedly, we still have some way to go in relation to waiting times – for example, for cardiac surgery, ENT, and ophthalmology, the proportion of people waiting longer than 12 months has fallen and we are making significant inroads on that over time. In relation to children waiting for cardiac surgery, the data shows a 67% reduction in the proportion of people waiting longer than six months.

One of the major reforms this year is the Treatment Purchase Fund, an organised way of referring work to the private system. 2002 has been the set-up year. I think if we look to 2003, based on the arrangements that are in place at this stage with the private system in Ireland and suppliers in the UK, there is capacity to put through 7,200 cases during 2003. The key determinant at this stage is the identification of suitable patients and the organisation of the necessary pre-op preparation and post-op support. In terms of the progress already made in 2002, it has proven to be one of our success stories and one that has, over the time that we are building up the capacity of the public system, the capacity to relieve some of the pressure and provide assurance for people depending on the public system that they will receive treatment within a reasonable period of time.

THE ACUTE SYSTEM: THE HR DIMENSION

I mentioned earlier that some of what we do under the other frameworks for change has potential for deep impact on the acute hospital system. The HR function – and all that we do around strengthening this function – is particularly significant in the acute hospitals, but also in primary care and continuing care. One example of an initiative here is the rapid expansion in the intake to various paramedical courses at third level.

Developments in nursing education provide another example of on-going quiet development. This involves a significant investment in expertise and new departments in universities, as one element of the follow-through to the Report of the Commission on Nursing some years back.

Some of the new ideas in the education and training of nurses – in particular, the development of the Specialist and the Advanced Nurse Practitioner grades -- will create new levels of competency within nursing that have not been present in our health system before. In order to gain value from these developments, we will need to take a more critical look at how clinical work gets done both in hospitals and in the primary care sector. We also need to look questioningly at traditional views of professional boundaries as we move through this change.

MEDICAL MANPOWER

The need for more critical analysis is intensified by taking account of developments nationally and internationally relating to the medical workforce. The exercise being undertaken by the National Taskforce on Medical Staffing, to my mind, has the potential for the most profound implications. Planning is underway to address the requirements of EU Working Time Directives for non-consultant hospital doctors, for the requirements for education and training and for fully recognising competencies that are developing in other areas.

If tackled constructively and imaginatively, the organisation of clinical work, when we are finished with this exercise, should never be the same again. The two pilot sites in the East Coast Area Health Board and Midwestern Area Health Board should prove to be testing grounds where practical questions get fully sorted through. The National Taskforce has been very busy and there is a lot depending on what they are doing in terms of the future of the acute healthcare system.

Some of the agenda items emerging underline the key importance of defining more clearly the role of particular hospitals, looking questioningly at working patterns, rostering of staff generally and skill mix. The opportunity to explore the idea of the extended working day in hospitals and to develop closer service integration should be fully grasped. Again, it comes back to closing the loop between the acute system and primary care and other aspects of the system.

ORGANISATION AUDIT

Another piece of quality work currently in progress is the audit of structures and functions. The brief here is to look at the scope for rationalisation, to look in particular at governance arrangements in relation to the total health system, and to look at the relationships between the multiplicity of organisations we now have that make up the total health system.

While this was planned for completion by end-2002, it will now be early 2003 due to a delayed start-up at procurement stage. The project is now well advanced and its completion should coincide broadly with the first report of the National Taskforce on Medical Staffing. The deadline for the Commission established by the Minister for Finance to examine financial governance in the health system is also early New Year.

It is likely to be around the recommendations from these various reviews that the precise shape and functions of a number of bodies announced in the Strategy will be formed. In particular, the National Hospitals Agency and the re-structuring of the Department itself will be in the frame.

INFORMATION FRAMEWORK

I made reference earlier to the Information framework. Implementation here is to be supported by a new Health Information and Quality Authority. Its brief is around three areas:

- The development of health information systems
- The development of national standards in relation to quality
- A national function in relation to technology assessment.

The Health Information Strategy has been prepared and will hopefully see publication in the first half of 2003. It will set down the framework for the Health Information and Quality Authority.

SUMMARY & CONCLUSIONS

Finally, let me summarise the key points of my analysis. In relation to both the primary care system and the acute hospital system, we are talking about high performance systems. Both systems are working under pressure. It is also the case that, in both systems, we are talking about the potential for a new order. I hope that some of the on-going and potential developments I have outlined briefly will have given you some impression of what that new order might involve. I believe that the significance and impact of the major reviews currently underway – particularly on structures and the medical workforce – will become clear in the near future. There is a genuine and far-reaching reform agenda being shaped around these projects.

Stronger dialogue is needed both within each aspect of the system, between the different parts of the system and increasingly between the public and private systems. I think, finally, the National Hospitals Agency will play a pivotal role in relation to the acute hospitals going forward, both in shaping the future additional capacity and also in carrying through the work that is currently being done by the National Taskforce on Medical Staffing.

III

THE NEW CENSUS DATA: RECENT DEMOGRAPHIC TRENDS & ISSUES

AIDAN PUNCH

SENIOR STATISTICIAN, CENTRAL STATISTICS OFFICE, DEMOGRAPHY DIVISION

I think that my paper provides the background for the way the healthcare system in Ireland is actually going. What are the factors impacting on it? First, a very quick look at historical trends, just to see how we have got to where we are at a national and regional level. I will also look specifically at the components of population change – namely, births, deaths and net migration (people both coming into the country and leaving the country). Finally, I will examine what sort of outlook is facing us going into the future.

Just to look at a graph you will all be very familiar with (**Slide 1**) – the population of Ireland from 1841 to the present day.

SLIDE 1:

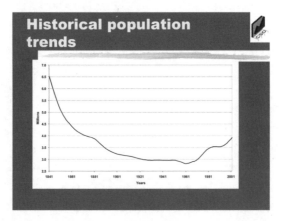

We can see that, for the area representing the Republic of Ireland, the impact of the Famine is very visible. There was emigration in the wake of that famine – we had a massive population loss, an even more drastic population loss than countries we know of that have suffered more recent famines. The population settled at around 3 million for around 30 to 40 years, around 1920-1950 – then you can see the graph dropping down during the 1950s, due to the outward migration during those years. Our population reached a low point of 2.8 million in 1961. What is important is what has been happening since – the upward shift in that population graph – and its key impact on the delivery of health services.

Moving on, **Slide 2** looks at the situation since the foundation of the State. Basically, there are three series: The natural increase is the difference between the numbers of births and deaths; Population change is the red line through the middle, whereas the bottom graph shows the net migration – that's the difference between inward flows and outward flows. So, where that is below the line, you are looking at net outward migration, which has largely been the experience here apart from the 1970s and also in the later period since 1991, and specifically in the last 6 years since the 1996 census.

SLIDE 2:

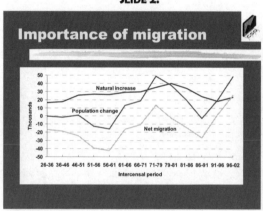

Overall, during that period, deaths have been fairly constant, running at between 30,000 to 33,000 a year, which has not changed much, even in recent times. So what is driving the natural increase in the population is the number of births per year. Births peaked in 1980, with 74,000 births in that year. There has been a downward shift in births since then. However, since the early 1990s, we have started to see an increase once again. The question is whether that increase going to continue into the future?

There is a popular misapprehension that fertility only started to decline in Ireland since 1980. In fact, fertility has been in decline since the 1960s. What happened between 1961 and 1981 was that the number of women in their prime child-bearing ages (20 to 39) actually increased by 50%. The number of births increased by 20% – so each woman, on average, was having fewer children. The total fertility rate declined quite significantly from the 1960s onwards.

Net migration, as you can see, during the 1950s, ran at a net outward rate of some 40,000 to 50,000 people a year. We saw a resumption of that in the late 1980s, when a lot of the people who were leaving were graduates who could not find work here. In the earlier period, emigrants tended to have a lower level of education. As well, a greater proportion of people in the earlier period went to the United Kingdom.

Very significantly, in the most recent period, we are seeing large inward migration – even higher than what we experienced in the 1970s. It is the combination of natural increase and net inward migration that is leading to the increase in the stock of our population every year.

Slide 3 looks at migration flows since the mid-1980s. The heavy blue line represents emigrants – in the late-1980s, emigration was running at 70,000 in some years. Many of those people were highly-educated young people, who had been through secondary and third-level education. A lot of these people have been returning in the more recent period.

SLIDE 3:

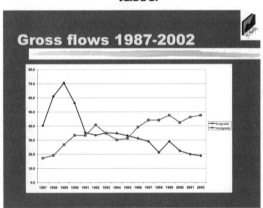

We did an exercise around 1990, where we looked at the censuses from a number of other countries. At that stage, there were close on 1,000,000 Irish-born persons living outside the State. The population of Irish-born persons living here at the time was about 3.5 million – so 1 million out of the 4.5 million Irish-born people alive in the world were actually living outside the country. A lot of those had clearly emigrated in the 1950s, because 700,000 were resident in the United Kingdom. A lot of those people will never come home. They have made their lives in the UK.

What we have been experiencing in more recent years has been outward migration of our more well-educated people and, to the extent that they can afford to come back and live here, they are coming back. That is become a big issue in these past five years. With our economic growth rates, the cost of housing has gone way up, so there is an issue over whether we will see a continuation of net inward migration. My own gut feeling is that it cannot be maintained at the levels observed in the recent inter-censal period.

The last Census, the results of which we published in July, showed the population of the State to be about 3.9 million – an increase of 300,000 in six years – up 8% in six years. There was an average annual increase of 1.3% *per annum* during that 6-year period. Compare that with the previous census period, where the increase was slightly over 0.5% *per annum*. Go back to 1971 to 1979, the first period on record where we had net inward migration and the population was increasing by around 1.5% *per annum*. To put this in context, we have been experiencing very high growth rates in our population, far in excess of anything being experienced by our partners in the EU or OECD.

The components of that change during the past six years are births running at about 64,000 per year, deaths running at about 31,000 per year, with the difference is of the order of 33,000. So we are getting a natural increase in our population which is stable and one which is going to be there well into the future, albeit declining, of about 0.5% every year. That is there, it is not going to go away, and we can plan for that into the future.

The population changed by about 50,000 a year – what we experienced during these past 6 years has been a annual net inward migration of 25,000 or thereabouts. When you consider that, on average, we would have about 20,000 emigrants every year anyway, you are looking at annual gross inflows of around 45,000.

SLIDE 4:

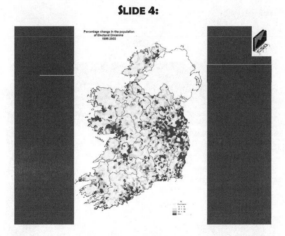

Slide 4 shows an interesting map, with implications for health services. It shows where people are located, and where population growth is taking place. But, with the population changing, there is probably a need to change our outlook about where health facilities need to be located.

The darker colour on the map illustrates a population increase of over 15%. Most of this action is along the eastern seaboard, as well as on all the radial routes out from Dublin. That is where most of the population change has been taking place over the past six years, as well as in other cities as well – Cork, Tralee, and

Galway. There also has been an increase in the number of people working in Northern Ireland, and living in areas such as the Inishowen peninsula.

The map paints a picture of change in Ireland. Ireland is becoming more urban, less rural. Leinster continues to gain population share, as it has done since the foundation of the State. That does not mean that the other provinces are not increasing in population – they are – but Leinster is gaining in overall population share.

I'll define urban first – 'urban' means people living in towns and cities with a population in excess of 1,500 people. So it is quite a restricted definition. What it shows is that back when the State was founded, 2 million of the 3 million Irish people were living in rural areas – Ireland was predominantly rural. By 1966, we had equilibrium in terms of urban/rural, and what we have seen since is that the population increase is being experienced in urban areas. The population of rural areas is flat.

On the map in **Slide 4**, the lightly shaded areas, which are areas that have lost population over the most recent six-year period – mainly in rural, western areas where no new houses are being built, where the kids have left to go on to third level or abroad – we are seeing declining populations in these areas.

In contrast, the larger towns are experiencing population growth. That is important from the point of view of delivering healthcare no doubt, and it is a trend that is continuing.

SLIDE 5:

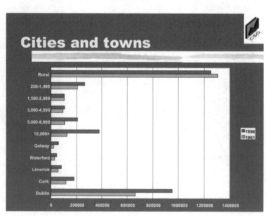

Slide 5 shows the same thing, but from 1961 up until 1996. It shows the major population centres – Dublin and its suburbs, a major increase there up from about 650,000 to nearly 1 million – and that's just purely Dublin and its suburbs, it is not taking account of the surrounding counties. Galway, Cork, Limerick – all experienced population increases. Towns of 10,000 or more increased in a major way. Towns of population 5,000 to 10,000 also increased.

The only areas where we have seen a population decrease are the rural areas. The population in those areas has actually decreased since 1961 (when the population of the State was 2.8m) compared with 1996 (when the population was 3.6m).

Let us talk about components of population change. I have already talked about the issue of migration, but clearly births, deaths and the ageing of the population are issues that also have a direct impact on the provision of healthcare.

In fact, speaking of that natural increase, and looking at the regional picture, there is a very solid result. In the earlier periods there, you see the dark bar, which was the remainder of Ireland outside of Dublin, Kildare, Meath and Wicklow (termed the Greater Dublin Area). If you take the rest of the country outside that area, what you saw in previous periods was that the natural population increase, with the number of births exceeding the number of deaths, was higher in the rest of Ireland than it was in the GDA. What you are going to see onwards into the future is population growth coming in the Greater Dublin Area, purely on the back of natural increase. So, even if you had no internal migration towards the east, or no flows from abroad towards the eastern part of the island, you are still going to get very strong population growth in the east of the country.

SLIDE 6:

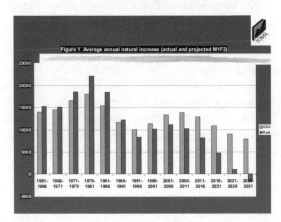

The reason is very simple. It has got the youngest population. Although fertility rates in the east are lower than they are in the rest of the country, its istill going to experience rapid growth from new births alone. So that is important as well in terms of where the population growth is going to happen.

Just, very briefly, on fertility – where does Ireland stand? As we can see from this map, Ireland stands at the very high side of fertility – in fact, Ireland has the highest fertility in the European Union. Ireland's fertility rate fell from an average of around 4 in 1960 – a woman of childbearing age between 15 and 49 had on average 4 children. It has been below replacement for over a decade now– there has been a slight pick-up in that recently, but nothing to get excited about as Iwill explain in a minute.

We are still below replacement, but yet we are on the high side compared to our European Union partners – in fact, we are the highest in the European Union. My own belief is that fertility rates will decline even more, and that will obviously impact on the number of births that are going to actually take place.

SLIDE 7:

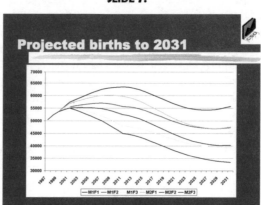

Slide 7 shows six scenarios going forward. These six scenarios correspond to the combinations of assumptions about migration, of which there were two, and fertility of which there were three. Statisticians are very cautious people – they rarely give you forecasts, what they give you instead is a range of projections.

I think the most important graph here is the third one down from the top. That shows that the number of births is going to increase temporarily above 55,000 and then it is going to start to decline. What we have been experiencing recently, and will continue to experience into the future, is a cyclical effect. Our births peaked in 1980, persons born then are now are in their early 20s, and in the early part of their child-bearing ages. So we are going to get that effect going forward into the future. But notwithstanding that, fertility rates are going to continue to decline, therefore the number of births is going to decline into the future.

A critical issue is the older population. If you look at, say, the population aged 65 years of age and over, in 1996, they numbered about 400,000 or thereabouts. The following was the strongest result of the projections exercise that we did. It really does not depend too much on migration at all. People who are going to be 65+ in the year 2030, a lot of them are here now. They are not going to leave. Most people who emigrate are in their late teens or early 20s. If anything, the figure may be on the low side, because it would be swollen by more people of older age coming back to Ireland. We have some evidence of that in the most recent Census.

The result was that the number of people aged 65 years of age and over is projected to more than double between now and 2030. This will have a huge impact on healthcare, on pensions and on a whole raft of other areas. The 'very old' segment (those aged 80 years and over) of the population will also more than double from 90,000 to 200,000 during the same period. Those projections are very robust, very strong and are not too dependant on the assumptions you make.

Where will these people live? Well, I can tell you where they have lived from the 1996 census. These were persons living alone in private households throughout the State. The total of persons aged 65 years of age and over living alone was 106,000. I gave you the figure of about 400,000 persons aged 65 years and over, so that represents about 1 in 4 of persons aged 65 years of age and over were living on their own in 1996. As we go through the age groups then, 70 years +, there were 28% living on their own; 75 years +, there were nearly 30% of those living on their own. In fact, old persons made up 44% of all persons living on their own – that figure will probably drop but the important question is what percentage of the older age group is actually living on their own. That has important implications for healthcare.

Slide 8 depicts dependency ratios – the number of persons aged 0 to 14 as a percentage of those aged 15 to 64. And then the number of persons aged 65 years of age and over as a percentage of the same thing. You can call the group in the middle the 'active' persons – although there is a case for making it narrower, perhaps 20 to 59 – but you get the same picture.

SLIDE 8:

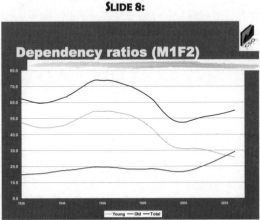

The other two age groups are dependant on the middle group – kids obviously, and often the older people too, even though they may have their own resources. What it shows is that we are living in a golden age at the moment, if you look at the blue graph. We are at close to the bottom of what it has ever been and what it's ever likely to be. It is going to get worse from here on in.

The reason it is going to get worse is that we are going to have more older persons. Look at the red graph at the bottom, the slope will be upwards – the green line is going downwards, reflecting what I said earlier about birth rates dropping. So, just to reiterate, we are living in a very good period at the moment, we should be making the best of it by making provision for the future.

IV

CHANGING DEMOGRAPHICS – THE IMPACT ON GENERAL PRACTICE

DR RICHARD BRENNAN

CHAIRMAN, IRISH COLLEGE OF GENERAL PRACTITIONERS

As a general practitioner, I am conscious that primary care and general practice provides 95% of healthcare needs to the population. Although the debate sometimes gets skewed towards the hospital sector, the majority of healthcare actually gets delivered through primary care. That really is the model that we should be considering, and it is also the model that will allow us to take some of the burden off our hospital system.

AN INCREASING POPULATION

My first point is the trend towards an increasing population. At primary care/general practice level, this immediately impacts on capacity. There are issues around general practice manpower – it is well documented that GPs are already very busy. We presently give around 18 million consultations *per annum* – mostly on a same-day availability and with a good degree of equity. It has been shown that if GPs get very busy, and if time is less available, the areas that are affected most will be chronic, psychological and social care. There will be a tendency not to deal with these problems and, as a result, referral rates go up.

Quality of care is very important. If GPs are very busy, time is at a premium. Not every issue can be sorted out. In Canada, where they are looking at the family practitioner networks – similar to our own model proposed in the primary care structure – the ratio they are aiming for is one GP per approximately 1,200 patients. Most of us in Ireland are still working on the ratio of one GP to maybe 2,000 to 2,500 patients. That raises the question of what sort of service do we want to provide? Do we want to provide an illness service or a health service?

The next question is who provides this service? Is it doctor-provided? Or nurse- or practitioner-provided?

Then there are issues around capacity and what sort of service people want. GPs will always put themselves forward to be the leaders of the team and to see ourselves as being central to the process. Perhaps that has developed as a result of the historical availability of GPs, and the under-funding of community support services in primary care, over many years.

While looking to meet the needs of an increasing population, it is important to remember that, in planning our services, they are patient-centred, and that we are responsive to the needs of the community. We must always remember that we are dealing with individuals – we are dealing with somebody's mother, brother or uncle. We must remember that especially when we look at impending financial adjustment. It is very easy to manage economies in one sense, without necessarily taking on or understanding the impact those economies have on an everyday basis to the people to whom we provide healthcare.

The other very important aspect with regard to an increase in population is the functional role of the GP. It is a pivotal role – the role as gatekeeper to the services. That is why I mentioned capacity issues – what can be dealt with in general practice should be dealt with in general practice in primary care. But, if the resources and the time and the structures are not there, what happens? The patients move. They move from the primary care sector into the secondary care sector.

If I can just illustrate that: there are approximately 2,500 GPs in this country. If, every day, every GP referred one extra patient into the system, that would be 40,000 patients a month extra into the hospital system. If they refers one patient less, that would be 40,000 people a month *out* of the hospital system. It is a very very important role we play. It is very important that, when we are planning and configuring the health services – and not just the hospital services, we must ensure that the resources are there in primary care. The capability to swamp the hospital sector is there if GPs inappropriately refer.

AN AGEING POPULATION

The second issue is an ageing population. By 2030, we will have doubled the number of people over 65. This brings its own set of problems.

Elderly people have a greater degree of complexity of care. They generally have multi-system diseases, higher consultation rates and greater prescription costs. There are different attitudes to illness in the elderly – years ago, it would not have been that unusual for somebody over 70 not to be offered bypass surgery simply on the basis of age. But family expectation and patient expectation now is that people want – and demand – the very best.

There is a question: is age an illness and what can we do about it? Because, on the other side of the equation, you have pharmaceutical companies developing, producing and investing in products largely around diseases connected to ageing. We can expect to see a huge increase in drugs for dementia or for other illnesses like that. I am conscious when I am looking at my prescriptions that, where previously an elderly person might have been on two or three prescriptions, they are now on seven or eight. They are on something for osteoporosis, they are on something for their memory, they are on something for their heart, they have their beta blockers, their aspirin, etc.

There are ethical questions we must ask about where we are going as a society. Also, when we talk about changing attitudes towards the aged, there is the question of who cares for the elderly person? I think there is a feeling that caring as a concept has been lost. People are too busy – economics dictate that young people are out working. The original family as we knew it has disappeared. There is no longer anybody at home to mind the granny or granddad, if he or she gets sick. The pressure on GPs is to move them into the casualty service, or the hospital service – move them any place, because we must be doing something. These are societal issues which we have got to face up to.

Equally, I think the other question that comes up again is the question of long-term care. Families are no longer prepared to mind elderly relatives at home, unless they have the appropriate supports. Those include community nursing, twilight nursing, availability of respite beds. A lot of people will mind their elderly relative at home, if they have the support. But, without the support, the notion will not be entertained – regrettably because we do not have the services. People have got streetwise. They have learnt how to leave a family member in casualty and walk away. That is to be seen in any casualty department any day of the week. People tend not to make themselves available, even to consult about the future.

As I pointed out above, the most important thing with regard to the ageing population is to ensure that they have access to, and the capability to avail of, community support services. We need to look at enabling people to stay at home. We must keep at the back of our mind, what does the patient want? Always, 99% of the patients want to stay at home – they want to stay in their own home.

Economically, it might be easier to put someone in a nursing home, but that is not what the patient themselves wants. So, community support services are needed – we need to develop more respite, and we need to develop more rehabilitation services. Especially with elderly people, there is a tendency that, when they have been diagnosed with an illness, to feel "that's that" and off they go to the nursing home. There's no more to be done for them.

I think we need to look again at elderly people – very often, illness in the elderly is episodic, and you can return people out of long-term care and back into their communities, given the right sort of incentives and encouragement.

The whole question of the ageing population means we need to configure them into the planning hospital issues, long-term care issues: Are there going to be community hospitals? Are we going to have sheltered accommodation? Are we going to encourage private development of nursing homes? That brings in the question of who supervises nursing homes? What quality of care do they provide? Or are they just a convenience to put granny out of sight?

Allied to encouraging people to invest in long-term nursing homes, we need to look at the provision of realistic carer's allowances. We should be enabling people to come out of the workforce and mind an elderly relative, even if only on a temporary basis. That provision does not exist – so a realistic carer's allowance, a remodelling of that whole area, needs to be looked at.

MULTICULTURISM

The next striking thing is that we are now developing a multicultural society. We have an increase in the ethnic mix: migrant workers, asylum seekers. This is not just happening in Dublin, but right across the country. We must understand that people have cultural differences to health and to expectations. There are language and communication problems on both sides – the doctors and care providers, on the one hand, and the patient on the other. There are different health needs – physical, social and psychological health needs – for these people and, to a large extent, we are probably not meeting them.

There are huge educational needs for GPs, primary care teams and the wider community in this area. We must prepare the doctors, the carers and the community to integrate these people. It is very difficult to defend situations sometimes, when a hotel may get redesignated as a refugee centre. Very often 50 or 100 asylum seekers arrive, often with no interpreters, with health problems, ringing the GP and expecting the GP to be able to sort things out. There needs to be better linkages between the Department of Justice and the Department of Health. There must be a better flow of information and better preparation to allow us to encourage and integrate these people into our communities.

The multicultural society, for some of the reasons, I mentioned earlier on will have an impact on secondary and tertiary care. Again, if it is a medical problem, it is likely that this patient will be referred on to casualty, or to a secondary care setting, and I am not sure that the services for these people in the secondary care sector are any better than they are in the primary care sector. So, this is an issue that we need to be cognisant of and to be working now at re-planning.

POPULATION LOCATION

Where we live, the problem of every young married couple: Where do you buy a house? Where do you live? The statistics again show an increasing population in the eastern region, and a decrease in population in the more rural areas. From a general practice point of view, it is interesting to see what happens. GPs – because they are self-employed independent contractors – will follow the business. When you look at the maps – and Professor Tom O'Dowd has done a very nice map overlaying the location of general practices and the city in general – you see straight away that the majority of GPs are in Dublin 4, Dublin 6 and Dun Laoghaire, and that we leave areas of the inner city completely deprived of GP services.

This is less of a problem in rural areas. With pride, I say I come from Kilkenny, where we were partly instrumental in developing CareDoc. I always like to remind people that CareDoc was, in fact, a GP initiative, aimed at providing cover and services for GPs and at recognising the fact that, with depopulation, we were finding it increasingly difficult to recruit people into general practice to work in deprived or rural areas.

While co-ops will help in some of the depopulated areas, they will not necessarily be the total answer. This is going to be one of the other key questions – the geographic spread of practices to meet the need. Do we continue to leave it up to market forces as to where people establish a practice? Or do we need to sit down and plan general practice disbursement across the country, so that we know that the needs of the people in each county are being met.

The whole question of dormitory towns raises commuter healthcare issues. How do commuters access their healthcare services? Who do they access it from and when? People are getting up at 0630 and they are probably not getting home until 1930 or 2030. Who do they get their healthcare from? Because, if they are away for the day, they are not getting it from their local practitioner. Do they go to somebody in Dublin? If they are seeing somebody in Dublin, do they need a second doctor for night-time cover? Do they have any continuity of cover? Again, these are issues we need to look at when we are looking at the sprawls we create.

I am conscious that, in Carlow, there is not a hospital. People in Carlow do not have access to a hospital casualty department. It has not been a huge issue because the development of the co-op has provided the availability of an emergency service. But, what we are seeing is people accessing the emergency service for routine care. That is inappropriate. It is the same as young people accessing casualty for their medical care, as opposed to coming to see the family doctor.

HOSPITALS

Lastly, I want to raise the question of the distribution and access to secondary and tertiary care. The hospitals, by and large, are becoming very centralised in Dublin and the major regions, and I think we are going to see a lot more of that. Communities do have concerns when they see their smaller hospital being downgraded. There is an important point here that, when we reconfigure our health services, the local community must be taken on board and we must be able to offer them an enhanced primary care service, if we are decreasing some of the hospital services that are available.

POVERTY & HEALTH

The statistics do not really show anything much about the socio-economic factors and health. But these are very important issues. Poverty and deprivation are really the key markers for health outcomes in this country. It is not whether you go to a doctor in single practice or group practice – it is poverty, and where you live, that will determine your health outcome. That is an issue that has to be addressed.

The question is one of eligibility of access. Within modern-day society, we have the so-called 'new poor' – people who have double mortgages, who are working but who defer their healthcare because it is that little bit extra that they cannot afford. There are a number of perverse incentives in healthcare. Sometimes it is cheaper to access healthcare from a hospital outpatient or casualty than it is from your GP. We need to identify these perverse incentives and inverse care laws and really target the service and make it accessible to people.

Most important, with regard to deprivation, is the development of community empowerment and getting people involved in their own healthcare. A number of issues have come up already today where we are looking at young people – at their increased smoking or drinking alcohol. Really the message has to be that parents have a responsibility with regard not only to their own healthcare, but also to the healthcare of their children. Part of the educational process here has to be looking at educating our future generation for parenthood and its responsibilities and educating our existing parents in how to mind and provide ground rules of good health and behaviour.

There has to be an integrated, multi-disciplinary, multi-agency, inter-departmental approach to issues like deprivation and provision of healthcare services. We cannot get enough GPs to work in the areas between the two canals in Dublin. There are no incentives. The cost of setting up a practice there is prohibitive, and doctors do not see it as an attractive option. When we are looking at these areas, we have to look at them in terms of environmental impact. People are planning new towns, new villages, refurbishing apartments – we need to have a multi-disciplinary approach. We have to be involved in there at the planning stage. And we have to create incentives for people to go in and provide care to the people who need it the most.

SUMMARY & CONCLUSIONS

A few brief points before I finish up. Traditionally, GPs have always been the first responders to changing demographics. Every time there was a housing estate built, a young GP went out and bought the house on the corner and set up his practice and worked from the bedroom. That was the traditional thing – but that is no longer the case. Our younger graduates are not prepared to do it.

The other part of the problem is that we are not getting the equal geographic spread required to provide a unified system across the country. We need to be aware that the extended primary care teams have been much slower at getting in to respond to the changing demographics. It has been easier for GPs because they are individuals and they are the owners of a unit of care – the bigger organisations are much slower. We need to look at how the health boards and communities identify health needs and how they respond.

We have an immediate need to increase GP numbers to meet present and future demand. I make no apologies for putting a pitch in here. We train at the moment 75 GPs per year. We have a need to train 150 a year. We need to train between 1,000 and 1,500 to meet the 10-year needs.

The manpower issue is very complex. I was talking to one of the tutors on one of the training schemes. By way of illustration, they did a 10-year review of graduates – of 36 who went through one of these training schemes, only 13 were in full-time general practice, 13 were in part-time general practice and 10 had left medicine altogether.

People need to be aware that, of the 75 GPs we are training each year, we are only retaining two-thirds in general practice, only half of them in full-time general practice. Hence, there is a degree of urgency about addressing general practice manpower.

As I indicated above, if we are not there to be the gatekeepers and providers of primary care, the burden will move directly on to the secondary care providers. That is simply what happens in real life. So, in terms of addressing the health needs of the country, we must ensure that we have an adequate number of GPs to meet these needs.

The average GP can meet 94% of the healthcare needs of the individual patient – as a statistic that applies across the board. Sometimes, and I have heard it said, the answer to the GP shortage is nurse practitioners. They have them in Canada, and in England, to meet the needs of communities where GPs could not be accessed. But the information at the moment tends to suggest that nurse practitioners can meet only 66% of the health needs of the individual, as opposed to a GP who can provide 95% cover.

I am not using this in any way to cast aspersions on the ability of the nurses. I think they have a useful role, which needs to be developed. But it should not be at the exclusion of developing a proper manpower strategy for general practitioners.

Allied to our numbers, we need to look at what work we do. We need to be aiming to reduce the average list size, and to increase the range of services provided in practices. We need to develop integrated care pathways within the community with our fellow workers who work in primary care and also within secondary care. We need better communications and IT links. We need better protocols of care. We need patients to have their care delivered at the appropriate level – hospital care should be episodic. Patients should go into hospital when they have a problem that cannot be dealt with through primary care. But the patient should then, when they are better, move out of the hospital system and back into the primary system.

That has been a flaw of outpatient departments for many years. There are a number of patients attending who do not necessarily need to be going every three months or every six months. Effectively, they are blocking access to other people who may need it.

I made the point that primary care had been under-funded for many years. General practice itself has been under-funded. We need to look at a system that allows resources in healthcare to follow the patient. Resources should be delivered to the system that delivers the care. The budgeting of healthcare is an area that does need to be reformed. Block budgets for institutions needs to change.

Do not underestimate the gatekeeper role of the GP and the factors that influence their decision on whether to make a referral into secondary care. I would just finally like to mention that the Deloitte & Touche study on Value for Money concluded that GPs are good value for money.

V

IRELAND'S CHANGED ECONOMIC OUTLOOK: KEY IMPLICATIONS FOR EXCHEQUER SPENDING ON HEALTH

ROBBIE KELLEHER

HEAD OF ECONOMIC RESEARCH, DAVY STOCKBROKERS

My task is to set out the overall economic background for the context of people who are involved in health policy over the next couple of years or so – both in a global sense and, more particularly, in an Irish sense. I want especially to focus in on the demand that is going to be there on Exchequer finances and Exchequer resources over the next couple of years.

I think, in the world we live in today, when you are looking to put together a view on any economy, we have to start in the United States. The US is, far and away, the largest economy in the world. It accounts for 40% of world output. It has been the key driving force behind the very rapid expansion most economies experienced in the 1990s. When you look around the world, there does not seem to be any other region in shape to take over that role. The other major regions like Japan are in very poor shape. Japan has been in decline since the late 1980s, and does not look like it is going to improve anytime soon. Mainland Europe looks to have chronic structural problems, and it too does not look like a candidate for taking over this 'locomotive' role that the United States has performed over the last decade or so.

The most apt way to describe where we see the United States at the moment is as an economy that is suffering one hell of a hangover from one hell of a party that they had in the 1990s. Unfortunately, the pain of the hangover is not going to go away quickly.

In the second half of the 1990s, the United States went on a spending binge. The consumer sector spent very rapidly, and financed it primarily by borrowing. The corporate sector spent just as rapidly on the belief that we were in a brave new world and there would be infinite demand for goods, and it would go on for ever and ever and it was worth building capacity to meet that.

The counterpart of that was a major over-appreciation in equity markets. The most extreme was in the whole dot-com Internet area. But, even in ordinary stocks, you had an appreciation in price that was quite unprecedented at any time over the last several hundred years. Eventually, that bubble was pricked. In equity markets, it was pricked in the early part of the year 2000 – and equity markets have been falling ever since. In the places where the real bubble was, we have seen declines of 80% to 90% in prices.

In the real economy, the hangover is that they are left with huge levels of debts as a result of the spending spree they undertook in the late 1990s. They have had to adjust to the new realities of the new century and, in the process, have had to adjust their debt levels.

The corporate sector in America has adjusted in a significant way, and it has had painful implications for job losses. We have seen some very large multinational companies instigating huge job losses right around the world. That process is ongoing and plays a significant part of the correction they have to make in order to address the very real levels of debt that have been built up.

The problem in the most immediate future is that the consumer sector has not made that adjustment. Right throughout the downturn that has occurred in the US economy over the last couple of years, the consumer has continued to spend merrily away. Initially, that spending was financed by reduced taxes, following the Bush administration's election to office. More recently, they are spending their house in a sense – like in Ireland and the UK, house prices are still rising rapidly in the United States. That is generating a lot of excess equity in houses, and people are borrowing that extra equity and using it to finance current expenditures. So, the consumer sector has continued to expand rapidly, and is continuing to hold up the US economy. We do not see that as sustainable. There have been some recent indicators – that suggest that the consumer is on the brink of making the inevitable adjustment to the huge levels of debt that were built up over the last number of years.

So, we see the US economy over the next number of years growing very slowly. That would be our best guess – that it will take three or four years to purge the excesses that were created during the late 1990s. That would be our central scenario. There is an alternative, which is one where the adjustment takes place much quicker, but is much more painful. I would have a slight preference for the more prolonged adjustment, that is not as sharp but takes longer, over what is called the 'double dip' – that consumer spending is going to contract, and contract very sharply, and will do so next year and we could get a severe recession next year.

I would not rule that out as a distinct possibility, but my best guess is that the world, led by the US, is entering a period of much lower growth rates than what we have been accustomed to over the past 10 years or so.

That is the background against which the Irish economy will have to operate. It would be highly unusual if the slowdown that has occurred in the global economy did not have an impact on an economy like ours that is so dependant on others. We all know that the years 1993 to 2001 were years of unprecedented growth in the Irish economy. We could spend all day explaining why they occurred. But, if you boil it all down, the key factor has been the success we have enjoyed in attracting American multinationals to come and locate here and use Ireland as a base to sell into European markets. As I mentioned, corporate America invested very heavily in capacity in the late 1990s; they did so not just in America but across the world as well. Ireland was particularly well-placed to attract such Foreign Direct Investment coming from America.

Given the problems that corporate America has, and given the slowdown not just in the American economy but in the global economy as well, it seems to me to be highly unlikely that the flows of FDI that we have enjoyed will flow into Ireland in anything like that same magnitude as they did in the 1990s.

I also think we will also get a smaller share of what flows are there. In the 1990s, we were particularly well-placed in terms of our age structure, our population structure, our ability to speak English, our tax regime and so on. Now the Central and Eastern European Union applicant countries are better placed to gain a bigger share of those Foreign Direct Investment flows from America.

So we are faced with a scenario where, firstly, the flow of investment form America into Europe will be greatly reduced in comparison with the late 1990s. Secondly, our market share of whatever flow does come will be lower than it was in the 1990s. That has huge implications for the Irish economy.

We believe at the moment that the Irish economy is growing at about 1% to 2% per year – I think it will continue to grow at this rate into next year, and perhaps into 2004. Medium-term, the sort of growth rate the Irish economy can generate will be of the order of 3% to 4%. That is the scenario.

Some people describe that as being a 'bearish' outlook – but I think that is an odd use of that particular phase. If we are capable of coming off a period of seven or eight years where we grew by 8% to 9% *per annum*, and we can go through a couple of years of 1% to 2% and then we can get onto the growth path of 3% to 4%, that is not such a bad outcome, although there are much more optimistic forecasts out there. Some people are forecasting 6% growth next year – a lot of medium-term projections are forecasting 5% to 6% growth into the medium-term. I think that is far too optimistic.

The basis for the more optimistic forecast is that what drove us in the 1990s is still here – we still have good demographics, we still have young people, we still speak English, we still have low taxes. Those factors were sufficient to deliver the high growth rates in the 1990s, they are still here today and they should be sufficient to do the same.

The point I would make is that demographics in the 1980s were not entirely different. There were lots of kids coming out of college, most of them spoke English, most of them were reasonably well-educated. Taxes were 10% in those days – yet all our people had to go off and get jobs. That is because the global environment was very different. Therefore I would be more cautious about where global economies are going over the next few years and, indeed, about the medium-term potential of the Irish economy.

I do not think it is a catastrophe. I do not think it is a total disaster. But I do think we have to reduce our expectations greatly compared to where we were in the late 1990s.

One of the consequences of the 1990s is that our understanding of what constitutes normality was fundamentally changed. There is a definition of a recession in the United States – if you get two quarters of negative growth rates, it is a recession. We have got to the point in Ireland now where, if the *growth rate* is less than 4% or 5%, we call *that* a recession.

Some forecasters who are predicting growth rates of 1% to 2% for a few years and then 3% to 4% are being castigated as being incredibly gloomy. That reflects an example of how people's perception of what is normal has been distorted by the 1990s. When we look back on the 1990s, the period 1993 to 2000 will stand out as a truly exceptional and abnormal period, both in terms of Irish economic history and in terms of global economic history.

To try and locate normality references within that context is a big mistake. The indications for the public finances, I believe, are pretty clear and pretty obvious. They have already manifested themselves. Both this year and last year, expenditure will grow by about 20%. Revenues will grow by about 4%. Now you do not need to spend several years in the Smurfit School of Business to figure out that that cannot last very long. We got away with it last year and, to some extent, this year because we are coming off a cushion of running a very big surplus. But we are in to running a deficit this year and, certainly, the arithmetic for next year looks to be extremely difficult.

Again, definitions of normality have distorted even the budgetary process. We have had the great McCreevy leak in the papers about cutbacks – and it transpires that, after all the cutbacks, public expenditure is still set to grow by 10% to 11% next year. That is more than the economy can afford. The economy in nominal terms next year will grow by 4% to 5%. Tax revenues will also grow by 4% to 5%. So, if you want to grow expenditure by 10% to 11%, then you are going to have to put up taxes, and start to put up taxes pretty seriously.

Again, we have got to get into concepts of normality in public expenditure as well. We have got to start defining what cutbacks are and are not. We seem to think that 8% to 10% would be a fairly vicious budget. The reality is in the medium term that public expenditure here will have to be constrained to grow by 4% to 5% – maybe 5% to 6% maximum – unless we are willing to shoulder some fairly hefty increases in taxes.

What that means is that we have to be focussed on Value for Money in public expenditure. Most of us, looking at things from a distance, see huge increases in public expenditure – it went up by 40% in two years. It is not obvious to a lot of people that we have gotten any great delivery in terms of improved public services out of that 40% increase in expenditure. That is the key of the debate.

Looking at things from a health perspective, I would not want to put myself up as any sort of an expert on the health system, but health expenditure has more than doubled in five years and, in terms of expenditure per head of the population, we are now well up there with everybody else in Europe. As a colleague of mine who is known for his wit said, given the amount of money we have poured into the health system, there should be a nurse on every street corner. But, you know, health seems to be an example of something where you just pour money into it and nothing seems to come out the other end.

That is the big challenge for the economy and for public services. We are into a world of low numbers – low interest rates, low economic growth rates and, in terms of public service, unless we are prepared to shoulder an increase in the tax burden, we are into relatively low increases in public spending. That is an environment where I think important rationalisations, decisions and trade-offs will have to be made. The period of the Celtic Tiger was a period where politicians gave up making choices because they did not have to make choices – they could give in to all the sectoral demands. That era has gone, and that is the big challenge for public services and, given the role that health plays within our public services, it is a bigger challenge for health than for any other sector.

VI

THE LACK OF COMPETITION & ITS IMPACT ON THE SUPPLY OF ACUTE HEALTHCARE

PROFESSOR MUIRIS FITZGERALD
DEAN, SCHOOL OF MEDICINE, UNIVERSITY COLLEGE DUBLIN

Professor Ray Kinsella: *Professor FitzGerald, what is the argument being made in this paper, regarding the need for greater competition in the public acute system?*

Professor Muiris FitzGerald: The core arguments are, first of all, that it is a failed system and that there is absolutely no evidence in the system of competition or incentivisation. The reason that this is the case is because the health system is highly politicised – so, before any arguments begin about the optimum methods of distribution of health resources, there are overriding political arguments, that particularly relate to the acute hospital sphere which consumes a very large amount of the money involved.

These political arguments are that our uniquely dispersed system of small, essentially unviable, hospitals must be preserved, because any threat to these uneconomic units will result in electoral disadvantage. Now, if the approach to the health system always begins from that point, then there is very limited room for manoeuvre. So therefore, there is a political stranglehold immediately placed upon any argument, or any initiative when it comes to dealing with the acute hospital service.

RK: *Are there any other elements that you would see as part of an overarching set of principles that impede structural change?*

MF: For the holistic delivery of healthcare to widely varying constituencies of need within the health service, you must have an in-built flexibility in the workforce. That is, you must tailor the job descriptions and the key personnel characteristics to the job to be done. However, within the Irish healthcare system, there are highly monopolistic influences on exactly what kind of healthcare worker can be employed and their exact conditions of service.

This again produces a stranglehold on the ability to respond in a versatile and flexible way to healthcare needs. It starts off with the fundamental fact that all the healthcare professionals are highly organised, highly unionised, and have very clear job boundaries and vocational boundaries contractually built in. This is inimical to any flexible healthcare delivery system that requires a holistic multi-disciplinary team.

The key emphasis in healthcare must be teamwork. To start with groups of healthcare professionals that are rigidly organised in a vertical fashion, as opposed to having very strong horizontal connections, is a great disadvantage.

With regard to terms and conditions of doctors in the hospital healthcare system, this is classically exemplified by a very rigid contract that essentially stipulates that to achieve a permanent post in the health service, you must have a particular type of consultant contract that has built into it several unique privileges. That means that the doctors who deliver healthcare essentially consist of a higher elite of what I would call five star generals, if we were to use the military analogy. Then there is a steep drop to a very large pool of non-commissioned officers, who do not have a permanent contract.

There are many other similar examples of such rigidity within the system. If you do not have a flexible workforce of highly trained doctors who are matched to the job that needs to be done, then your ability to deliver a responsive, sophisticated healthcare delivery system is greatly impeded.

RK: *In the introduction to the National Healthcare Strategy, there is an analysis of the benefits of competitiveness. But one of the anomalies is surely that this does not extend to the healthcare delivery system, where there is a significant absence of competition and competitiveness?*

MF: That is absolutely true. The National Health Strategy, in its introduction, mentioned competitiveness only in respect of the way that the country's prosperity has evolved, and it paints a picture of a health service that does not perform, while the economy remains competitive. Nowhere, however, is there any mention of the same dynamic that was responsible for our national Celtic Tiger economy having a place within the most conspicuous consumer of those benefits – namely, the Health Service.

You would imagine that the same dynamics that contributed to our success in one area could be translated, probably with modifications, into the healthcare system. But, if you look at the National Health Strategy, there is virtually no mention of the word competition, and only occasionally does one see the word "incentive".

RK: *Given the importance of incentives in the competitive model, particularly in the Celtic Tiger era, why do you think there is such a lack of emphasis on incentives? Is it simply a system that is unresponsive to change?*

MF: It is absolutely true that there is a dearth of any true competition within the healthcare system. There are various forms of sham competition or limited competition – but these are few and far between. With regard to the education of health professionals, that is going to reap a very negative dividend for these reasons.

First, by not professionalising the education of health professionals during their undergraduate years in university – and now virtually all healthcare professionals are educated within universities – the investment in education has been stultified by an assumption which goes like this: healthcare professionals are educated on university campuses relatively cheaply, and that component of their education requires a relatively small input – approximately €8,000 per head, and then for about 50% of their education, they go to the healthcare system where they get what is often called a free apprenticeship.

This is entirely out of kilter with international trends, where healthcare professionals are educated with a marked clinical component right from year one. This requires very significant resourcing, but in Ireland we have the very peculiar tradition where the Department of Health indicates that the education of health professionals has nothing to do with it. They contend it is in the education domain – whereas the posture of the Department of Education is that, while it has responsibility for the education of healthcare professionals while they are on university campuses, the moment that they cross the threshold into a healthcare facility, they have no responsibilities.

As a result, we now have a situation where healthcare professionals attract a capitation payment per annum of €8,000 – whereas for medical students in the University of Glasgow, it is €36,000 per healthcare professional. Now this is an example of where there is boundary issue and a failure to take responsibility for an integrated model of health education.

Finally, the reason why this is not just an undergraduate issue is that a key dynamic in retaining the best and brightest of our healthcare professionals in Ireland, is that they, in their postgraduate years, must have an equally sophisticated training system. But, at the present time, we have sub-optimal investment in post-graduate education, thus prompting some of the most talented individuals go abroad for the preponderance of their training, leading to a net loss from the State.

RK: *Would you agree that, in talking about a competitive paradigm, we are not talking about profitability or shareholder value, rather what we are saying is that a competitive model has a key role to play in improving equity, access and in improving healthcare outcomes?*

MF: Broadly speaking, yes. The present situation is that there are virtually no incentives, except perverse incentives, within the healthcare system. There is also a lack of competition – much of which derives from deliberate under-capacity in the hospital sector. There is no incentive, when you have a capped hospital budget, to increase productivity. There is every incentive to discourage customers from coming to the facility. Those that stay away benefit you more that those who come. Everything within the present system, particularly when it has under-capacity, leads to an anti-competitive model and a highly disincentivised model. The normal incentivisation system regarding increased productivity does not occur within the health system simply because there are no rewards. If I can give an example of the effect that under-capacity has in a system when it comes to incentives: If you try harder in an incentivised system but have no capacity to increase your output or meet your waiting list targets, or see more clients, you do not even begin.

RK: *If we take the two parts of what is essentially one system – that is the public/private mix – we see on the PHI side regulatory barriers stemming from a very dirigiste system that has, in effect, kept out insurers who could play an important role in this capacity building. Now this seems to resonate with the lack of competition that we also see in the public sector.*

MF: Certainly, if you have restricted capacity, you only have one recourse and that is to set a maximum of activity. Clearly, a maximum is reached quickly and that then immediately creates a barrier to output. The issue in private health competition is slightly different to the public health service. The private system would always contend that it is in a competitive stance within certain niche areas of medicine, such as elective surgery. When anything is very acute, the private system generally indicates that it does not have the capacity or the specialised resources to deal with that activity. So, sometimes, there can be slightly naïve comparisons made between the public system and the private system, as if they were providing the same portfolio and array of services. They are not. But the argument still holds that, if you restrict capacity, you create immense difficulties – whether it is public or private.

One of the slightly perverse starting points of all health service arguments in the public sector in Ireland is that it is politicised. Otherwise, you could not explain why you have a network of very small hospitals that have few parallels in other developed European countries. For example, Mallow Hospital with 54 beds, Bantry hospital with 68, Nenagh with 68, Cashel specialising only in surgery in a town of 2,900 people with 75 beds – and the list goes on.

These are not viable units. But so many people make a virtue out of these small hospitals and say that they provide local services, they respond to local needs and are therefore competitive. However, the very minor virtues of those arguments are completely negated when you find that these hospitals are not just looking for a niche area of medical activity. They want to have acute 24-hour full services in most of the mainline disciplines of medicine and surgery. Now that is absolutely unsustainable from the risk management point of view, from the sustainable development point of view and from an economic perspective.

All of this dysfunctional hospital configuration is maintained by intense political lobbying. A hospital in a small country town is not regarded purely as a healthcare facility. It is a local industry with a lot of economic dependence on it – so that the medical arguments, the safety arguments, the risk management arguments all become subsidiary to that one local imperative.

Because of our multi-seat constituencies, there is a dynamic that maintains these hospitals, even when, quite patently, some of them cannot function effectively. In reality, there is no need for that particular political posturing. These healthcare facilities can have a viable future if they reconfigure and re-profile the array of services that they provide. These smaller hospitals can provide excellent community-based services – the things that people in the locality most frequently need – but they need to divest themselves of the high-risk areas such as modern high-technology surgery, some of the more equipment-intensive and expert-intensive sub-specialities, and do what they are good at – delivering local community services at a high standard.

But locally this is regarded as downgrading. The view is that, unless you have the full all-singing all-dancing hospital, you have been downgraded and some other town has gained at your expense. This results in the complete paralysis of efforts to construct good regional centres throughout the country. That is the perverse dynamic of the multiple small hospitals in the regions, vying with each other in sham competition, leading to an outflow of patients to Dublin, Cork and Galway. If all of these individual hospitals came together with the right profiles and configurations, you could establish excellent regional centres that could bring sophisticated services closer to the individuals in that region.

RK: *Two questions: First, whether the increased evidence on risk management, and the failures we have seen in risk management in recent years, is not now at the point that would impel some sort of dynamic towards a regional system? Second, whether you believe that the new primary care multi-disciplinary teams being promoted by the Department of Health might complement such a regional system of smaller hospitals?*

MF: I think that the primary health care system is the key linkage is absolutely vital in reconfiguring the small hospitals. The model that I think would work would be one where, in communities that have small unviable general hospitals, there would be an agreed profile of appropriate local community services delivered in tandem with consolidated primary healthcare practises that come together in organised groups. In this integrated model, you have all of the benefits of fully qualified doctors in the primary healthcare system, working in teams with doctors in the local small reconfigured hospitals, to provide a whole array of services right across the spectrum from the simplest primary care problems to local day-care surgery, specialised outpatient clinics and geriatric and rehabilitation services.

In that environment, where already within the primary healthcare system you have a public/private mix that is more vigorous than in the hospital system, you certainly can introduce incentives, you can introduce competition, in a way that is virtually impossible if confined to a small local hospital.

The interaction between the primary healthcare system and the hospital system at a local level will permit two things to happen: One is a patient-dictated array of local services that is instantly accessible by incentivised groups of healthcare professionals who have a strong motivation to provide a better and more comprehensive local system of care. At the same time, you can have the additional benefits of having a nearby high-specification consolidated regional hospital centre that will deal with problems of greater complexity and also deal with problems which, in risk management terms, can only be provided where there is a critical mass of specialised personnel, modern equipment and facilities and up-to-date modern information technology.

RK: Could we go a little more deeply into the advantages of the model? If we have a multi-disciplinary primary healthcare service working in tandem with a network of smaller hospitals, it seems to me that what comes out of that is improved screening and primary healthcare services that keep people out of the acute system – which is obviously a lot more cost-effective. Second, there would be improved primary service communication so that, when people do go into the acute service, it is again much more cost-effective. This more flexible primary care regional hospital network system would also help prevent the huge overload there is on the Eastern Regional healthcare system at the moment. It would actually deliver, for all the regions outside of Dublin, a much more balanced healthcare system. I wonder if you might also spell out the disadvantages of seeking to maintain this network of hospitals which, as you say, are unviable and are both draining resources from the national acute system and also not delivering a patient-outcome oriented service even at the local level?

MF: With our current network of small hospitals dispersed over a wide geographic area, the first thing you are doing is spreading resources very thinly. You cannot therefore develop specialisation. You are forced, in this model, to configure a generalist consultant delivery system that can do a lot of things with reasonable competence but where you cannot provide specialised capabilities, such as sub-specialist care and sophisticated 'diagnostic services'.

Because you reproduce this generalist model in multiple locations, you then reduce the amount of money available to spend on specialist services – which then are only available in the Eastern Regional Health Authority, in the Southern Health Board/Cork region or the Western Health Board/Galway Centre. In that flawed system, you give a less specialised service to the regions by spreading it thinly in a dispersed small-unit generalist model and fail to consolidate it in at least one good regional centre with a high specialist profile. Essentially, by maintaining a network of five hospitals in a health board like the North-Eastern Health Board, you block the development of a competitive regional centre which would will provide an array of services to match that provided in a large urban area like Dublin.

What that means is that, in a particular region characterised by several small hospitals, you promote major regional outflow. Patients with any significant complex problems immediately go outside the region. The local view is that "I'll fight in the trenches to preserve my small local hospital, but if I develop anything of even medium complexity, I'm going to bypass that hospital and go straight to a major centre outside of the Health Board region". So there you see the slightly schizoid approach adopted.

One of the most important additional elements is that it wastes resources. First, when hospitals are jam-packed in the large urban metropolitan centres, there are vacant beds in some small county hospitals. So, in fact, if you look at the percent bed occupancy of a portfolio of small hospitals, you will not infrequently find empty beds, while, elsewhere in the system, there is total under-capacity.

The next and very powerful argument against these small hospitals providing a full range of 24-hour in-patient services is that, if the amount of work being done is not sufficient, then you are creating highly expensive rosters of all health professionals. If you look at such work practices over a 24-hour period, you would be paying premium salaries for cover – not for care. In other words, professionals cover the service in case people require services. You are not paying them for actual work done. In our present system, where junior hospital doctors and many other healthcare professionals attract very expensive premium overtime payments, paying for cover rather than care is an expense that we cannot afford. By contrast, in a large regional centre, where the high patient demand is there, when you pay premium payments, you are actually paying predominately for care, and not just cover. That is a very important economic and efficiency argument.

The next issue is risk management. It is just not possible to provide a sufficiently safe system for patients, in an environment where, for complex surgery, surgeons do not have the volume of the cases that is needed to hone and maintain skills on a lifetime basis. This is a key element that will eventually close down certain types of specialty activities for hospitals. So, if the politicians will not do it, the risk managers will – and that is inevitable.

Finally, if you look at the profile of recruitment of junior hospital doctors to peripheral hospitals, what you find is that in some health boards, there is the truly amazing statistic – that 90% of the junior doctors have never trained in Ireland and come from the India-Pakistan subcontinent. They come in expectation of getting good training, and end up being disappointed because these small hospitals are not recognised for validated higher training. So, what you do is you staff these hospitals at great cost to the country, but also at great cost to the doctors that you bring in, because their expectations are not met.

The plethora of small hospitals in every region represents a balkanised system that tragically inhibits any attempt at implementing a national or regional health strategy. A good example of a national health strategy that has been compromised is the National Cancer Strategy, where a local divvy-up of some of the fruits of that initiative resulted in piecemeal dispersal of cancer-related specialists – one each for hospital A, B, C and D – whereas they should all have been appointed for integrated cancer care in a single cancer centre in a region. So, local politics has resulted in the divvy-up of cancer services to satisfy local constituency needs, with the result that no effective coordinated regional cancer policy has been instituted.

RK: *Can we just nail that last point? What seems to be coming across is a model where you have national centres of excellence and co-existing alongside them a regionalised system of viable local hospitals, together with a new multi-disciplinary GP centre, all working very closely together and giving superior outcomes, more cost-effective and better use of capacity, improved patient outcomes, and a more flexible training system in terms of medical manpower which, of course, is particularly important to the whole issue of accreditation. Could you comment on that point, and also maybe on what needs to happen to persuade people to adopt this model of a regionalised system, instead of the present political game?*

MF: Well, just to reiterate that vital concept of a continuum of service provision in a linked system, where you have a new upgraded fully resourced primary care system, intimately linked with the network of small reconfigured local hospitals to provide an appropriate array of community services, and then linking in with highly-resourced large regional centres and supra-national centres. This is the only way in which you could have an integrated care system where each problem is dealt with at the level of most appropriate complexity. That then prevents you from having the anomaly of people going for low-complexity operations from, say, the Midlands to Dublin hospitals.

But the issue of training and accreditation is absolutely crucial. If we are to have a flexible array of the most appropriate specialist expertise available to patients, we have to make an investment in their training. That starts at undergraduate level, and then in a continuum goes to post-graduate specialist education. This lifelong continuing professional development and education can only occur based on regional or national centres of a certain critical mass.

So, in addition to a service provision continuum, I would use the same paradigm for an educational continuum – from undergraduate training through to the practising professional. In Ireland, one of the key investments we must make is in an integrated programme to sustain that educational continuum. At the moment, it is completely fragmented, it is under-invested in and we see a large number of more talented people going abroad because they will not tolerate being trained in institutions that, if they do not now, will, certainly in the future, not have appropriate accreditation.

RK: *What is your view on the most visible sign of structural problems in the community healthcare system – namely, waiting lists? Surely it cannot be right that 10 years after the first Waiting List Initiatives, we are still working within the framework. Instead of the Waiting List Initiative being a temporary measure while we solve the structural problems, we seem to be bedding it down. Equally, the National Treatment Purchase Fund seems to be a form of temporary system to allow the public, for reasons of greater equality of access, to buy in to the capacity of the private system. Would it not make more sense to acknowledge that there is simply one system that could be much more closely integrated, simply because the same service* is provided covering both? Do we also need to work on the supply side, to enhance the capacity of the private sector so that it can be used both by those who wish to have PHI cover, but also that same capacity can be made available to other patients?

MF: First, we have Waiting List Initiatives. But these are never bid for between institutions – largely because, they do not have the capacity. So, what we have is what I would regard as a kind of sham incentive. Essentially, it goes like this: a particularly troublesome, often politically explosive waiting list, such as eye operations or hip operations, is identified. The monies are added into a hospital's global budget on the basis that x number of hip operations or eye operations will be delivered. Certainly, in a system that had the extra capacity, that would seem to be a reasonable strategy. However, what in fact happens a lot of the time is that when you favour one particular group of patients, ring-fence the beds for them, ring-fence the operating theatres, what you are effectively doing is excluding and displacing another group of patients.

So, that is why I think there is an element of sham in that kind of selective waiting list clearance. Next, let us look at the National Treatment Purchase Fund. If you have a public health system and a private health system that, on the whole, does not have enough capacity, and then, if you further know that the consultants in the public and the private system are virtually one and the same, because of the public/private mix, that "competition" between public and private is very limited, and can actually produce some perverse incentives.

For example, if a consultant in the public system is told that if his waiting lists go above a certain level his patients will be sub-contracted out for care in the private system, that same consultant actually may also be the provider in the private system. There are significant ethical and equity difficulties with that model. So, again, the issue of supply-side and the under-capacity limit the benefits from competition and incentivisation.

RK: *The issue of sustainability arises here: In other words, the affordability of the public acute system, that seems to focus more on constraining demand rather than increasing supply, or of availing of supply that would be available on the private side, in order to improve equity and accessibility on the public side. What, in your view, are the main barriers to a more competitive type of model, which would involve both the public and the private system, since they both, in effect, function as one unit, both from a service provider's point of view and from a consumer's point of view?*

MF: Well, the first thing is that there has to be better capacity. That is a given right from the beginning. The difficulties with the same providers being the providers to the public system and to the private system does create some ethical and equity dilemmas. When the providers from the public system and the providers from the private system are distinct and are in true competition, you do not tend to have that kind of ethical or equity problem.

Essentially, in the public health system, there is no tradition of competition.

There is no tradition of incentivisation – it is actually all in the opposite direction. If you have a capped global hospital budget, that means your potential for added productivity is greatly limited. You can have a huge capacity deficit in the large urban metropolitan system, where there is 100% occupancy, which indicates that there is no room for expansion – not to mention the inherent huge risk management problems. The barriers to competition also include inflexible staffing profiles in the public system, compared to the flexibility that you see in the private system. One of the areas where it is patently obvious that the private system can respond to certain types of need is the whole area of elective surgery. The reason that it can respond is that it is capable of getting over some of the labour constraints by having more flexible incentivised work practices where the elective capacity of an operating theatre is not confined to 0900 to 1700 five days a week. A private hospital will say "Yes, we'll put these through, we'll work longer hours and we'll work Saturdays". They have a flexible array of staff who will work within that adaptable system. Go back to the public health system and that degree of flexibility just does not seem to exist. There is no incentivisation within the system.

RK: *It must be extremely difficult for consultants – who conscientiously work extremely long hours, both in the public and private system – to cope with the reduction in capacity we are now seeing as a result of the focus on controlling demand.*

MF: It is a dilemma that every consultant in the public health system who has access to private practice confronts every day. There are numerous examples in all our large public teaching hospitals of public waiting lists for surgical and medical consultants who are willing to clear the list but cannot get access to public outpatient facility spaces, cannot get good support service and cannot get access flexibly to operating theatres. When they see that lack of institutional response to patient needs, despite their willingness to involve themselves fully, you can see that the public system is actually acting as a deterrent to many ambitious consultants who would like to provide more public services. There appears to be no flexibility, when it comes to providing that extra capacity through more flexible work practices.

RK: *The total employment in the health service has grown from something in the order of 60,000 to 90,000 over the last five or six years. Is the balance correct between, on the one hand, increases in front-line clinical, medical and nursing staff and, on the other hand, increases in administrative and management posts? Second, in relation to medical manpower, what is your view of the two main components – that is the lack of consultant facilities and, equally, the problems on the non-consultant hospital doctor side?*

MF: Well, in respect of the differential expansion of the managerial groups and administrative groups within the system, compared to the frontline professional, there are significant concerns that there has been a proliferation of middle managers. Now, we have the need, for example, for Risk Managers in large institutions on a highly professional basis. What people are concerned about is not that – that is absolutely appropriate – the worry is the proliferation of multiple managers where the need for the post and the potential benefit to the health service is often not very clear.

If you throw into the equation something that we keep going back to all of the time, if you also have to reproduce expensive managers on multiple small dispersed hospital sites, again, what you are doing is you are over-administering the system, rather than increasing management expertise. You are producing more of the generic administrative class, where the justification for those posts is debatable and in a highly dispersed system where the economies of scale just do not operate. That is a serious concern.

With regard to consultants – there are two things I would say. One is that we need a lot more consultants. They need to be consolidated in teams on regional hospital sites, where they can have appropriate rostering, where they can have the benefit of conferring with colleagues, and where they also reap the benefit and the educational dividend of attracting the best and brightest of Irish doctors in training to these large urban and regional centres.

Also, in conjunction with the national initiatives under the HRB, the Programme for Research in Third Level Institutions and Science Foundation Ireland, we can also retain these individuals by creating centres of excellence where, not only do they gain their clinical skills, and get the appropriate specialist education, but also have access to a research ethos – whether that research is in areas of fundamental basic research, or whether it is in the equally important area of clinical or health services research, it does not really matter.

However, in my opinion, consultants will have to change their contractual stance, which, at the present time, appears to lay people to be somewhat inflexible. Lay people perceive that there is only one type of consultant. There is no gradation, there is no system of incentivisation, there is no pecking order, there is no system of advancement or promotion on the basis of ability, or on the basis of contribution to administration, education or research. There is a flat hierarchy where every consultant is a five-star general. We must have a more flexible, trained, consultant workforce. We cannot carry on with a system where there are only two types of doctor in hospital practice – one the fully-trained doctor of a certain rigid specification, termed consultant, and the other the trainee. Economically, risk management-wise, and from a professional development point of view, that system can no longer continue. Medical organisations will have to show much greater flexibility in addressing the bizarre and inflexible manpower mix that we have at the moment.

RK: *Let us just turn briefly to the issue of the hospital doctors working in local hospitals – and, in particular to the incentivisation that exists because of the paucity of a wide range of resources. What kind of threat do you think this poses to the public system?*

MF: The public system is characterised by a whole series of disincentives. But the most spectacular disincentive is best illustrated by what confronts a newly appointed consultant who comes into the public health system, who has probably trained in some of the best centres abroad and who is coming back to contribute expertise for a professional lifetime to the Irish public system and to be involved in the private system as well, given our public-private mix.

In the public sector, in the large urban metropolitan hospitals, the majority of consultants do not have an office, they do not have a dedicated secretary, they do not enter an organised departmental structure. Almost immediately, they are reminded of the history of the public health system, which is that it was a charity-based system. They are expected to go into the private sector as an individual contractor, set up their own private consultation business off-site, and hire their own private secretary. Thus, their first encounter in their new job incentivises them to locate preferentially in the private sector. There is also an additional huge problem where there is under-capacity in the public hospital system. Highly trained specialists will frequently enter a specialist hospital and be told that they cannot have access to operating theatres except on an extremely limited basis. The under-capacity of the system results from the flooding of the hospitals with acute medical emergencies that fill most of the beds and prevent more specialised activities – whether they are diagnostic or surgical – from taking place.

So, you have a situation where highly trained specialists cannot carry out a sufficient number of specialised procedures and operations in their hospital because of under-capacity. Clearly, this is a huge disincentive within the public system. There are doctors who wish to work exclusively within the public system, but there is no incentive for them to do that. These doctors then clearly see the only outlet as being in the much more flexible incentivised environment of the private system, and that is the only way that some individuals can keep up their array of specialist skills. There is also a further structural disincentive within the public system in that many highly trained specialists who come from centres abroad to spend their professional lives in Ireland will have been used to working within a teamwork framework. This has the added benefit of colleague cover, rostering and so forth. In the public system, with a lack of any kind of organised departmental structure, there is a further disincentive built within the system.

Another disincentive is that many of these highly trained consultants would have spent a considerable period engaged in training high-echelon trainees abroad to a very high standard. When they come into the Irish system, there is nothing in their contract that obliges them to do anything in the educational sphere. Properly organised educational infrastructure is not present and there is under-investment in advanced training of junior doctors in Ireland. Here is a squandering of a huge resource – namely, the inability of newly-appointed consultants to have appropriately resourced protected time and facilities for training undergraduates and keeping talented postgraduates within the system.

RK: *The development of the Irish economy, since 1960, has been predicated on the importance of competition. Incentives are an integral part of that competitive market model. Equally, the case for competition has been well set out in the Taoiseach's Task Force Report on Better Regulation. Now, taking the case for competition, and in particular the case for greater incentives, what is your view on how this case for competition could be applied to the Irish acute healthcare system?*

MF: Well, firstly having got rid of the sham competition and reconfigured and re-profiled our hospital network, models of competition should evolve based on a system of bidding and tendering for programmed extra capacity. This is on the basis that the flexibility for extra capacity within the existing system is relatively limited. All the international comparisons show that the number of acute beds in the Irish healthcare system is well below that of other jurisdictions, to a very significant extent. So, extra capacity is crucial. I think this is where a new incentivised and competitive system would unleash a new dynamic. The worst possible approach to this would be to say that, across the country, largely for political reasons, we will put in non-specific extra capacity – a few beds here and a few beds there. We know that that is not going to be effective. The proposed competitive tendering model is not a sort of "extra capacity dole" that will be given out co-equally to each institution along traditional lines. This new method would be a more dynamic form of capacity building, where institutions have their competitive potential unleashed by being told that there will be bidding and tendering for, for example, a new state-of-the-art day-care facility.

Clearly, in that kind of situation, there is a totally new incentive, that has never been in the system before. To those who say that this will not work in the Irish system, I would say that all you have to do is look at what happened in third level education where the same dynamic was unleashed. The State, opting for the knowledge economy as its future hope, put a large amount of money in to open competitive research bids with matching funds coming from philanthropic organisations and private industry. In a period of three to four years, that approach entirely revolutionised the way in which universities deal with modern challenges. It threw off the shackles of a lot of outmoded procedural protocols, the constricted thinking of the old system, the boundaries established by rigid faculty systems and, instead, the universities adopted a competitive stance, where only measured performance was the indicator of success, and "winners", not second-rates, were rewarded.

Those changes to the education system resulting from competition would be multiplied by several factors within the health system. There is a huge dividend there if you unleash that competitive potential within the system. Bidding for extra capacity, linked to a revised array of vital services, linked to national strategy and patient need is the central strategy.

RK: *The concept of competition in healthcare, and the tendering for incentives, resonates with the UK experience and may possibly cause some unease among patients and healthcare professionals. What argument can be deployed to demonstrate that, in fact, in talking about a competitive model and improved incentives in the public system, that what we are really talking about is improved patient outcomes – as well as a more cost-effective system?*

MF: I perfectly understand the initial reaction – that this could be a flawed model because a particular type of internal market system in the UK failed. They tried to create a highly artificial type of internal competition that, in the end, was anti-competitive. They did not start by saying, "We have an area of very significant verified patient demand that remains unmet. We can codify and categorise it, and then we can target extra-capacity that institutions can bid for, in order to discharge a local, regional or national health imperative, without compromising other priorities in the process. If we adapt this starting-point and strictly monitor the process, we are adding something into the system that was not there before. We are linking the funding of targeted extra-capacity with the national health strategy based on an analysis of need, employing strict rules of the game, which then unleashes a constructive competitive posture between institutions to bid for this extra capacity. Successful institutions will benefit from this by realising the full potential of their staff by demonstrating their capacity to respond to health challenges and by adding to the expertise, facilities and enhanced reputation of the institution." Put simply, an institution adds to its prestige as a model centre of patient-orientated excellence and innovation by successfully bidding and delivering health targets that benefit patients and the community.

RK: *The model that we are talking about here essentially is aimed at a more patient-centred, physician-driven system, rather than the kind of* dirigiste *command-and-control model that is there at the moment. Would this proposed model be consistent with, for example, the government splitting its role as funder and also service provider?*

MF: First, with regard to the notion that this model might be centrally and managerially controlled, I think this is safeguarded by commencing at a starting point that nobody else seems to be starting from – the patient. First comes analysis of patient needs and then a projection of what is required to meet those needs. It does not start off by saying that x hospital, on average, should have 35 more beds in a traditional carve-up. The proposed model starts off by saying "Out there in the community, there is a need for the following services for patients with defined needs. Here is how we are going to meet those needs in a targeted way. Bid for this."

So, it is a different starting point than, say, generically building new facilities. It starts from an analysis of patient needs, and works forward from there. In that kind of system, where the patient imperative drives it, doctors will naturally be in the vanguard of the determination of priorities and the most targeted way of delivering these. This is an expert job to be done by the experts. It will require managerial input, but it does not start with managerial input, it starts with patient need and links it to the people capable of meeting that need – the professionals.

RK: *Finally, could you summarise the needs that are there, and how best to optimise the competitive advantage? Clearly the competitive model has a key role to play in building up a patient-centred system. How do we go about optimising this model, and how would you summarise what changes are needed to our acute healthcare system?*

MF: First, if we are to optimise competitive advantage, there has to be an attitudinal and a cultural change. The present system is highly codified, rigid, full of boundaries – moats and drawbridges at every turn. The only thing that will kick-start a process of change is incentivisation. We must prioritise the provision of extra targeted capacity – and have agencies bid for it.

The second thing that has to occur is the professionalisation of management. Sometimes, I alienate some of my good friends in management, by saying that there are lots of famous Irish doctors, but there are few famous Irish healthcare managers. There is an element of truth in that.

We have to have the highest possible level of management within the healthcare system. Many would say that the best models of management within the current system are those that work on medium-term contracts, with built-in incentives linked to patient-centred productivity. We keep coming back to this. Management must have a symbiosis with a group of dedicated health professionals who wish to make a major contribution by partitioning their job into management and some clinical care commitments, so that they can be a reality check in the system as well as a reassurance to colleagues on the ground.

Finally, no incentivised system will work if you have a rigidly codified workforce who only work specific hours under specific conditions and with specific privileges. We have to look at the flexibility of the workforce performance. That will involve contractual reform. There will have to be a broader portfolio of trained doctor posts – we cannot go along with a doctor system that is based solely on permanent consultants and rotating trainees. We should introduce incentivised contracts, and we must embed a team ethic into the system, as opposed to the "lone ranger" ethic that we have operating at the present time.

In summary, what I would say is that we really lack competition in the public system. We lack incentivisation. We have too much "perverse" or "sham" competition. To overcome the barriers to true competition, we need attitudinal and cultural change. We've got to have a targeted increase in capacity. We must reconfigure our manpower to make it more flexible. We must introduce incentives that are linked to national targets and outputs. While we have a public/private mix, there should be an incentivised system within both, where individuals would feel comfortable being in either system and free of current ethical conflicts.

RK: *One final question. We need a road-map to develop and kick-start this new model. We have to start with the Department of Finance, which controls the funding of the public sector. We have to work with the Department of Health and Children, which has worked very hard in recent years to produce a strategy. We have the health boards. We have the professional bodies. Whose responsibility is it to kick-start this process of reconfiguration of the public system?*

MF: I have no easy solution. This is a multi-faceted problem and an inter-agency problem. This must be a pan-sectoral approach, with an over-arching authority of some kind that would be different from the traditional systems that were plagued by political interference. There must be a strong international external input, as well as internal expertise from right across the spectrum of management, health economics, professional bodies and patient advocate groups. There must be some degree of budgetary control, naturally, but operating within a system that is still incentivised, with a competitive ethos and aimed at nationally-determined targets.

VII

THE IMPACT OF CUT-BACKS & EXPENDITURE ADJUSTMENTS

DENIS DOHERTY

CHIEF EXECUTIVE, ASSOCIATION OF HEALTH BOARDS, AND FORMER CHIEF EXECUTIVE, MIDLAND HEALTH BOARD

My working title for this paper was '*The New Economic Climate – Strategic and Management Challenges Facing the Health Boards*'. The reason is that it seems to me that through tough times, good times and approaching tough times, the big issues have remained the same. What I am going to do here is deal with some of those big issues, as I see them. I am going to do this by posing questions for society and opinion leaders more than just for the health services constituency.

Some of those big issues are around growing demand, the intended purpose of investment in healthcare, and what return we expect to get from it. Very relevant I think to the issue at hand. But first, I would like to deal with the very important issue of inadequate investment in our health services. Another question gaining greater importance as time goes on is the issue around staff recruitment and retention.

These big issues are not unique to our system. They appear in every discussion on health services in every developed country. I could pick a number of examples, but this one seems to be particularly apt for this country. A recent issue of the *Harvard Business Review* asserted that the health insurance system in the United States is broken, business is paying the price, employers' insurance premiums reached an estimate $450bn in 2000 and have since been increasing further, at three times the rate of inflation, in 2001. If that sort of thing is common within the healthcare system that spends more than any other, it perhaps puts some of our own problems in context.

I think the context within which the big issues exist is changing. The National Health Strategy, the Primary Care Strategy, the Cancer Strategy, the Cardiovascular Strategy and the Value for Money reports are all significant in their own right, and taken together amount to a significant body of work.

In the very near future, we are going to see the report on Financial Management and Control Systems, the report of the Audit of Structures in our health services and the National Health Information Strategy. They are all due before the end of the year. That body of work, together with the strategy documents I have already mentioned, are important in the context of our consideration of the purpose of this investment in the health services, and what sort of return we expect to get from it.

New procedures, new technologies and new patterns in illness are driving increases in demand. That is happening in primary care as much as it is happening in secondary care. It is happening in the caring services, and in the child protection services.

Nobody should have to wait the length of time some people have to wait at A & E Departments. Of course, the waiting lists that stretch as far as they do, in some cases, are unacceptable.

But again, in that context, our stock of acute beds is among the lowest in developed countries. The average length of stay in our hospitals is low by any international standards, and our use of day procedures is high by international standards also. The much-debated waiting lists amount to the equivalent of 2% of annual throughput. My question is whether that constitutes a crisis?

For the greater part of the year, hospitals have to cope with what used to be termed the 'winter bed crisis'. This year, the winter vomiting bug did not abate until the summer and reappeared in September. That, in a hospital setting which, by common consent, is 3,000 beds short of the required number. The first of those new beds will only be commissioned shortly. When taken in conjunction with that, the need to restrict admissions and to isolate large portions of hospitals has a major impact on a system that at the best of times is very short of beds.

There is one important area, however, where fall-off in demand has occurred and is a cause of significant concern. There is a whole generation of young parents who have no appreciation of the devastating effect diseases such as rubella, which have been controlled by immunisation programmes, can cause. The reduction in the take-up rates of immunisation is a cause of serious worry to epidemiologists who fear that some of these illnesses will reappear. The financial and cost implications of an outbreak of some of these illnesses would be devastating – not to mention the impact on the individuals and families concerned.

It seems to me that this raises a significant issue around community solidarity *versus* individual choice. At the moment, it seems that the individual choice constituency is winning out but it would be highly unfortunate if it were to continue to the point where the realisation comes only when we have a significant outbreak of an illness that really should not occur in this day and age.

However, that is but one of the issues that I think needs to be debated. What is the purpose of investing in our health service? The biggest issue of all in that regard, in my view, is what is the intended purpose of investment, public and private, that we make in healthcare, and what return do we expect to get on these investments? When politicians and commentators ask what we get for all this extra money being put in, it warrants an answer.

I have been a long time in the health service. I have not a notion really of what those who make those decisions at the political level expect by way of return on that investment. It seems to me that it raises the important question about whether we are willing to engage in serious consideration of concepts around investing for social return, and managing for social result, because all of the discussion in areas such as social services tends to be around investment for financial return, and managing for financial result.

We need to develop the ability to go that stage further and consider what is the purpose in social terms? What is the investment purpose in terms of social result? As managers, what social result are we expected to produce? I think we are entitled at least to be engaged in discussion on that.

In very simple terms, 65% of that extra money went on extra salaries and wages. Was that the intended purpose of that investment? And was the return what we expected? I do not know the answer.

I think, at the overall level, the issue of hospitals is going to continue to dominate the debate, even though it may not be the most important in terms of answering the question of what is important in terms of investment in healthcare. But, if the political imperative is to maintain every hospital on the existing landscape which has its origins in developments which took place 50 or 60 years ago, then we need to ask what requires to be done in order to deliver a modern acute healthcare service. What cost will be attached to that? We simply cannot deliver a modern acute care service from the present network of public hospitals. If we are to put a modern network in place, what approach are we going to take in terms of rearranging that landscape, or are we going to pay the inevitable price that is associated with an *ad hoc* approach?

The body of work I referred to earlier ought to enable those who represent our community to develop approaches to the development of our services over the medium to longer terms. The history of the past 25 to 30 years ought to have taught us that the strategies we adopt need to be robust against uncertain economic futures. I am a great admirer of Peter Drucker, and it seems to me that Drucker's definition of strategy as that which 'enables organisations to be opportunistically creative' is very apt in that context.

The health strategy aims to develop a world-class service, built on the principles of equity, equality, accountability and people-centeredness. That term 'world class service' is open to an infinite number of interpretations. I wonder whether we can chart an easier-to-understand course from the considerable body of recent work I referred to earlier and the other evidence and guidance at our disposal. Are we ready, I wonder, to take the longer-term strategic approach to tackling the problems of ill-health. As a society, I would suggest, we have not so far shown the level of commitment necessary to make a real difference. Are we, as a society and as a healthcare system, willing to commit to the level of sustained investment in health promotion that is necessary to achieve real progress over time?

Decisions that come from government, and which suggest that adjustments be made in areas not likely to impact on direct patient services, reinforce the perception that avoiding short-term pain is more important than achieving long-term gain. I wonder if that is a reflection of the priorities of the society that sees healthcare as a sort of breakdown-and-repair service. Does the community actually expect or demand, with all this money going in, a nurse or a doctor on every street corner? It may well be that there is more truth than we like to admit in that. That possibility recalls to mind something that Dr Asval, the former Director-General of the World Health Organisation, used to keep reminding us of. He used to say that those of us who know have an obligation to inform those of us who need to know.

If all that is required is a breakdown-and-repair service, I would suggest that can be accomplished in the short-term by diverting money from other areas. It can be accomplished, but it is more like fishing the bodies out of the rivers story eventually – there will be so many of them that the system will be overwhelmed by that too.

That would be a simplistic approach – as simplistic as the oft-asked question, why we need 11 Health Boards for a country that has a population the size of Birmingham, which has only one health board. The fact is that Birmingham and the Black Country has a population of 2.4 million and, in fact, have 29 statutory health authorities. Scotland has recently reorganised and has reduced drastically the number of health boards. For a population of close on 5 million, it has 20 health boards. And in the province of Saskatchewan, whose health care system is often put forward as one of the best, there are 10 health boards for a population of 1 million.

The point is that these are legacies of history, and they have their origins in different cultures and different approaches and, in terms of the quality of the health care system, structures matter not a lot.

I want to move on now to talk about the lack of investment in information technology. One of the major difficulties we encounter in seeking to have an informed debate on our health service is the fact that our information sources are so poor.

In the United States, they spend 2% of their significant healthcare budget on information technology, and have concluded that they are spending not nearly enough. That figure of 2% appears to be the norm in developed countries. We are currently spending more on IT than at any time previously, but that spending amounts to a half of one percent. This therefore is only a quarter of what is being spent currently in other systems.

The Value for Money report identifies this as a major issue. Indeed, those who are more familiar would not argue with the notion that we are under-investing to a factor of 10 or maybe 15 in that respect. So a major investment in IT in the short term is absolutely essential.

Furthermore, since it is unlikely that capital grants are going to be available to fund the investment, we need to find alternative ways of being able to make that investment upfront and pay for it over 10 to 12 years, which seems to be the norm around public/private arrangements around information technology. I have no doubt that until we begin to make that kind of investment in IT, we will continue to have these futile debates about what we are getting in return for the investment we are making.

That whole area of information is one where clinicians and managers, epidemiologists, politicians and commentators, all use the same information, but we just happen to look at it differently. Data is produced in clinical practice – and any clinician would welcome having clinical support systems at their disposal on a par with the best that are developed in places like John Hopkins and the Mayo Clinic.

That sort of clinical information – when aggregated and analysed – informs population health planning; it informs performance management judgement. By investing only a quarter of what other health systems do, we forfeit the opportunity to convert all the data we produce to knowledge.

Arising from all that, we are very poorly equipped currently to benchmark the performance of our system against other systems. Though, having said that, the benchmarking exercises conducted by the OECD and WHO in recent years portray our system in a much more favourable light than commentary on the system at home might suggest.

I want to turn now to my final point, which is around the recruitment and retention of staff. I happen to be one of those who believes the statement that staff are our greatest asset is a truism, rather than just a slogan. The reason I believe is not just because the number 90,000 is significant in itself, but really because of the skills, the experience, the judgement and most of all because of the wealth of knowledge they possess.

Studies reveal that people join the health services and the health system out of a commitment to society, out of a desire to care for the sick. They expect to be well-paid for the important work that they do. Just as importantly, they expect to be valued by the society they serve. These considerations apply to health promoters and health educators as much as they do to doctors, and they apply to administrators as much as they apply to nurses. But the reality is that staff not involved directly in providing services to patients feel less valued than those who do. That perception, I suggest, is contributed to by requirements communicated that adjustments be effected in areas which do not impact on patient care. Administrators and managers are often portrayed as an unnecessary overhead. Very often, little effort is made to understand why their numbers have grown.

A lot of that increase has come about as a result of the implementation of the Cancer and Cardiovascular Strategies, where those involved in health education and promotion areas were introduced from the health professions on salaries analogous to the clerical/admin rates. Because information was collected, analysed and published in a particular way over the years, it is not surprising that there appears to be a disproportionate increase in that area. It is also significant that when the recommendation of the Nursing Commission was implemented – the one that said that clerks should be introduced to take clerical work away from nurses -- that then became a cause of complaint about the number of clerical staff that gave rise to.

What I would like to emphasise is that there is a need for more understanding around what the real issues are in those areas. The sheer volume of negative coverage of the health services is having a demoralising effect on staff in all categories and at all levels. Talented staff we can ill afford to lose are availing of options overseas or outside the health services. It has become more difficult in recent years to fill positions at senior management level in general management and in the professional service area.

Now that we aspire to becoming a world-class health service, we need to have in place, and maintain, a world-class workforce. That in turn will involve placing greater priority on workforce planning, people development and people management than we have seen up until now. The health service is what Drucker would define as a knowledge workforce. It is not possible to increase rapidly the size of a knowledge workforce. It is very unfair to a knowledge workforce to downsize it quickly because of a downturn in the economy.

In this country, the health services have figured prominently in public debate. Almost inevitably, debate is rarely confined to the issues and very often focuses on those who deliver the service. When the health services are the designated battleground in political contests, I think it is important that some regard be had to the potential negative impact that sort of debate can have on those who deliver an essential service. I think it is particularly important in that context that, for the first time in our history, we have a skills shortage in our health services. That skill shortage is not going to be remedied, certainly in the short-to-medium term, even if we do increase dramatically the numbers we are training.

We need to view that, in the context of Britain and the United States having an enormous skills shortage, requiring hundreds of thousands of healthcare professionals over the next 10 years. That is going to offer opportunity to staff from here who may find it more attractive to work in other health systems, and the net effect could be a further negative impact on the skills levels here and the kind of consequences that Dr Brennan alluded to in terms of shortages in general practice and in primary care.

So, workforce issues have been equally controversial and problematic in times of plenty and in times of scarcity. I believe that a knowledge workforce delivering essential services is entitled to a clearer expression of what is expected from them in times of plenty, and in times of scarcity, than they have had available to them in the past.

The following conclusion was arrived at by John Harvey Jones following work he did across the public and private sectors in Britain. He concluded that 'managing a health service is an almost impossible task, and even if you did manage it almost perfectly, I still think the system needs more money'.

That was 10 years ago and, if anything, the task of managing the health services has become closer to impossible in the meantime.

VIII

MEDICAL MANPOWER – THE KEY ISSUES IN THE NEW BUDGETARY CLIMATE

DR COLM QUIGLEY

PRESIDENT, IRISH HOSPITAL CONSULTANTS ASSOCIATION

The problem: first of all, manpower. It is a lousy term – because the changes that have taken place in medical education involve 50% of medical graduates being female. That is going to impact on work practices into the future. Its impact is already being felt. Females do not see the point of working 90 hours a week and feel it is important to have a life. Also, they want to have children at the appropriate time. That is extremely unreasonable of them, but it is forcing change in the way practices occur in our hospitals and in our health services.

So, medical staffing. 450-ish, ballpark per year; we have 2,500 plus a couple of hundred other GPs, we have doctors in public health and in occupational health, 28,000-ish nurses, 3,800 non-consultant hospital doctors – but, of course, we import an awful lot of people from the Indian subcontinent and elsewhere to run our hospitals. We are not self-sufficient. We are actually totally dependent.

In-post at the moment, we have actually close on 1,400 consultants to provide the hospital services. Now, based on the November 2001 Bedstock Review – eight Health Boards at the time, 55 hospitals, 12,274 beds. We were 4,000 beds short – that figure has now dropped to 3,000. But probably 4,000 short of the requirements compared to European averages.

Now, the history, we lost beds, we lost investment in terms of keeping up with requirements. You know, technology costs enormous amounts. T-scanners, MRI machines – a million a go. Costs of replacement are enormously expensive. Twenty-seven years ago there were 1,000 consultants working in Irish hospitals. We have had an increase of 27% over that period – that is all – 1,400 now.

The National Health Strategy, outlined by the Minister and involving the National Hospital Agency, is hoping to address these deficiencies over the next decade – 3,000 beds needed. We have heard Michael Kelly talking about the first 700 coming through by January / February 2003. These are not extra beds – these are beds that are needed at the moment. If you wanted extra beds, fine, but these are actually beds that are replacements for ones that should have been invested in over the past 15 years.

We face realities – fine. If there are going to be cuts or realignments, Robbie Kelleher's point is very important. Where is the value for money? Well, the embarrassing fact is that, in Wexford hospital up to two years ago, we did not have a CT scanner, a basic piece of equipment for an acute hospital. I would be embarrassed to have to explain to a colleague from another European country that the people of Wexford raised IR£400,000 to get that scanner. The Health Board, to be fair to them, matched the funding 50% -- but it was the local people who got the scanner, not the health services. It is still operating a 0900 to 1700 service, so if you have a head injury after 1700 you have to go elsewhere for your CT scan. That is the reality – in 2002!

Layers of bureaucracy worry us, because John Given of the Irish Health Authority pointed out that Irish health boards and Irish health authorities do not use the same systems. It is not just investment in IT – it is also to make sure the systems talk to each other.

There has been a very significant investment to increase staffing in the health sector – that is very important. We now have, for the first time, caught up with and surpassed OECD averages for health workers in this country. So, we have got the staffing in place. However, we have the lowest number of acute beds per 1,000 of the population of OECD countries. We have the lowest length of stay. We have the lowest number of hospital consultants per 1,000 patients. Our bed days and elective admissions reflect the shortage of capacity in our system.

Okay – we are only cutting back on *planned increases* in expenditure. But the problem is that society has to accept that it has been misinformed by all political parties on what is possible. It is not just the government, but all political parties. Our politicians, as our representatives of society, have to accept responsibility and decide where healthcare funding takes its priorities.

To be fair, I take this from the *Irish Times* – figures from the Department's planned cutbacks. If you look at the incredible amount of money being spent on health, it is only a €50m readjustment that health is suffering – compared to, for example, Education. The only place that was not suffering was Transport with a zero cutback – everything else was cut by something. But health as a percentage – it is about a half percentage point, it is fairly small in terms of the overall realignments.

The pressures on GPs are not just to do with demographic changes. Society expects – and rightly so. It expects the best quality – now. 'I'm sorry your CT scanner is broken down – that's not good enough. Your CT scanner doesn't work after 1700 on a Friday afternoon and won't open again until Monday morning? Why?' I have to explain that to people, not an administrator. Not anybody else. The patient and relatives rightly expect quality of care. Quality assurance for hospital doctors, consultants and all other doctors from next January will become part of our ability to continue to practise over a five-year period. If you do not prove your continuing competence, you will be unable to continue practising.

Hospitals will have to become accredited – no problem with that, except we do not have enough hospital consultants to deliver the service that people expect. We have the second most litigious society in the world. Our healthcare is not that bad compared to Germany and France. Yet, in terms of litigation, it is the single factor that haunts everybody working in the health service – particularly where you are responsible, with your name over the bed, for that person. If anything goes wrong, your neck is on the line.

There are the concerns that medical indemnity is now becoming impossible to sustain. €450,000 would be the market price to insure an obstetrician in Ireland by MDU figures. The MDU have left that market. A neurosurgeon's price for medical indemnity doubled a couple of weeks ago. The market in Ireland in terms of insurance is coming very close to being unsustainable, unless something happens in the near future.

That is the reality that people who have responsibilities for patients are worried about and face on a continuing basis. The impression is that there are checkbox folders everywhere, but a lack of nurses and beds. The impact of reduced NCHD hours are going to be enormous. It is a legal requirement, and the slave labour conditions that went on will have to be dealt with. They are being dealt with but they are going to impact on our ability to deliver. We do not have enough consultants to meet the demand.

One neurologist for 400,000 people in the Southeast, for example, is a joke. The number of neurologists or brain specialists in this country is embarrassing in European terms. We have deficiencies in terms of our ability to deliver that no OECD country would regard as sustainable.

We await the Report of the National Taskforce on Medical Staffing (the Hanley Report).

Now, the problem for hospital consultants is that we have a duty to society to deliver – but we have to remain advocates for the patient. It leads one to a certain conclusion that you cannot acquiesce in cutbacks or realignments in beds or expenditure without making clear why. The reason for this may be Justice Quirke's High Court ruling, where a consultant obstetrician was judged on two factors. First, on whether his medical care was appropriate. The judge found not guilty – that was not the term used, but that was exactly what it meant. And the second factor – the consultant was judged on whether he acquiesced in a poor standard of delivery by the hospital concerned and whether the services available were of an appropriate standard. And he made it very clear to that doctor that if he, the Judge, found that that doctor had not informed the patient of inadequacies in that hospital, that he would have found the doctor guilty. He did not, and the case, as it turned out, was found in favour of the doctor.

But the striking issue was that doctor was found not guilty because he had demonstrated that he did not acquiesce in attempts to reduce standards of care. Irish hospitals are good – if you can get access to them. We have no surge capacity – we cannot cope with any extra surge. Yet we are going to face increasing demands. So, whatever the beds that are put in at the moment, they will meet the increased demand that we face now, but they will not catch up with historical deficiencies, and we still will have no surge capacity.

That figure of 1,400 there should be about 2,000 to 2,200, if we are going to meet Scottish levels. We are never going to catch up unless we really start increasing numbers from now.

A thousand extra patients attend acute hospitals each week, either as outpatient visits, casualty visits, daycare or inpatient care. That is 50,000 a year. Our activity where 1,400 consultants are legally-named responsible people – sued in their own name – responsible for a huge number of patients each year. We do not have the capacity to cope. We cannot provide the quality of care needed in 2002 in the quantity demanded by society.

Just to remind ourselves – second lowest number of beds, short length of stay, lowest percentage of admissions, and the highest bed occupancy. That is where we stand. We have constantly said over the last few years that 1,000 extra consultants are needed. It is going to be necessary for society at large to grow aware of our deficiency in consultant numbers. We cannot expect to deliver the care they need.

I will leave you with this chastening thought for any hospital consultant or for any doctor – that there is a certain duty to the individual that, for us, has to take precedence over our role in terms of State delivery. The Department of Health and Children, the Health Boards are charged by society to deliver healthcare to society as a whole. Each individual doctor must still remain the individual patient's advocate.

IX

IS THERE A QUALITY CRISIS IN HEALTHCARE?

HILARY COATES, SRN MBA
ROYAL COLLEGE OF SURGEONS IN IRELAND,
RCSI EDUCATION & RESEARCH CENTRE, BEAUMONT HOSPITAL

I am going to ask a question: Is there a quality crisis in acute healthcare?

But, before we look at that, we must look at what actually is 'quality'. If it is a transformation in the way we think and work together, in the way we value and reward and measure success, do we have quality in our health services? If we look at it as a customer's determination, and if you take the patient as the customer, based on their experience that the quality is measured against their requirements whether stated or unstated, whether it is technically operational or entirely subjective, and always representing a moving target in the professional market, do we have a crisis?

When we look at quality in healthcare, it is very important to realise that there are three different dimensions to quality. As the debate on quality has developed, thinking has changed about the definition. Quality in healthcare is a complex concept with many different components, the importance of which vary depending on the perspective of those involved.

Healthcare professionals are largely concerned with the safety and technical aspects of healthcare delivery. Policymakers and service providers have an interest in more population-based measures of healthcare, such as equity of division, equality of access and cost-effectiveness of the care provided.

But patients and consumers, while obviously concerned about these aspects of care, value other aspects of care such as information provided to them, the communication between them and healthcare providers, the ease of access to services, and the surroundings in which the healthcare is delivered.

I very much liked this definition I found recently that patient-consumers first like to be treated as a person, rather than as a disease. So, when you are looking at all those different dimensions of quality, it is hard to know if we have a crisis, and from which perspective are we dealing with it.

If we are going to look at whether we achieve quality in healthcare, whether accessible services are provided in an efficient, cost-effective and acceptable manner, and whether they can be controlled by those providing it. I think we need to view it in terms of structure, process and outcome. So, do we need to look at the resources – do we have the resources and facilities available for care delivery? What about the processes that relate to the actual delivery of healthcare, in terms of practice and procedures. That looks at the skill of the people giving the services and at economic assessments of effectiveness and efficiency.

Finally, it is important to look at quality from an outcome perspective. If we are looking at money we spend, we ask what are we getting from it? So we look at measures of morbidity, mortality and consumer satisfaction.

If we look at resources – do we have the resources or do we have a crisis? We have heard today a lot of figures being bandied around. The reality is we spent €8bn on healthcare in 2002. In real terms, over the last five years, that is a 70% increase in our funding. That is a lot of money. We have invested in people. We now have 87,000 – yet another figure – employees in the health service – a 28% increase. People should not be categorised by whether they are administrators or nurses or doctors or support teams. In fact, only 17% of health service personnel are actually administrative or management; 66% are engaged in frontline posts. So, the majority of our people are in front-line posts.

From a capital investment perspective, we have had an increased investment in buildings and equipment over the past number of years. We have a €497m investment in 2002, and an extra €2.5bn from our National Development Plan. But are we selecting and employing our resources in the most efficient way to meet our customers' needs? This is how we are judged on quality. Are we investing in those social results?

From an efficiency perspective – and we have heard a lot about the decreasing number of beds – yes, between 1980 and 2000, beds decreased in Ireland by 5,033. But despite this reduction in bed numbers, the number of in-patients treated has remained remarkably constant. Again, the number of day-cases have increased by 38%. From that perspective, yes we are giving a quality service.

We are looking at increasing our bed capacity: €43m was dedicated to waiting lists. Now, I also know that €50m was taken away because of our inability to spend it.

The question really we need to ask in relation to quality, is what about the patients who have been assessed as clinically fit for discharge from acute hospitals, but are still awaiting an appropriate discharge? Where are they going to go? What about those facilities? What about people awaiting outpatient appointments? Are we measuring that as a measure of efficiency?

When we are looking at outpatient appointments, as the population has increased gradually over the past 20 years, so too have visits to outpatients. We now have 2 million people visiting outpatients every year. Are they being appropriately referred? Why are they not being discharged from outpatients, back into a more appropriate setting in the community? These are the questions we need to ask.

Quality and fairness very much stress the need to ensure the provision of high quality and safe care at the heart of a modernised Irish health service.

Consistent with this, the Minister for Health has given the accreditation project his full support. The introduction of this scheme provides Irish health agencies with an appropriate mechanism, through which they can objectively measure and assess their performance against an agreed set of standards. But accreditation does not demonstrate whether a service has an effective quality system. That is something we have to take care of if we are looking at quality.

From a safety perspective, it must be recognised that no treatment is risk-free. Safety of course should be recognised as the first dimension of quality. So, how safe is our system? Well, we do not have the IT infrastructure in place to answer that question, so we sometimes have to look at lessons from other health systems. There have been a lot of studies done – the UK carried out a report on organisation which showed that 10% of patients incur adverse incidents as a result of clinical error. In the US, they showed a much lower rate – 2.9% – with a 4.4% rate of adverse incidents, of which 53% were preventable.

So, what does that mean to us here in Ireland? We do not have any figures of our own – this is not to suggest that we should reinvent the wheel. But if we just extrapolate that data from the study with the lowest results, it would imply 937 deaths as a result of preventable clinical error every year in Ireland. That is something we have to look at when we are looking at quality.

If we move on then to outcomes – in Ireland, the death rate due to pregnancy-related causes is 6 per 1,000. It is the safest place in the world to have a baby. Our infant mortality rate is very low. From an outcome perspective, yes we have a quality service. We do not have a crisis.

Again, we have heard much about morbidity and the fact that, even though our figures are higher than European norms, they are decreasing. We are putting in the structures for that by our Cardio-vascular Strategy. Again, our Cancer Strategy has supported these figures – so there is a decrease. So, outcomes – yes, they are quality, they are improving.

Michael mentioned the Irish Society for Quality and Safety in Healthcare National Patient Perceptions Study of 2000. We repeated that study and got the opinion of 4,000 patients who have had an intervention and we are currently analysing that data. The preliminary data analysis indicates a very high level – 95% to 97% – of patient satisfaction. So should we all clap ourselves on the back and say 'Well done'? It is important to note that perception depends on your conscious expectations and your unconscious assumptions. So, when we ask patients, we should take this into consideration. And, for patients, when we are looking at quality and defining quality, the quality of the technical and clinical care is a given, they should not have to question that.

So, to the question, is there an acute crisis in healthcare? Well, I do not know if I could give you the answer. But, looking at work done by John Oakwright, who showed that supplies are unavailable, work frustrating and staff suggestions ignored, followed in turn by undervalued staff, efforts ignored and poor quality is no longer noticed. There is increasing scepticism and resentment. You suddenly begin to see patient and client dissatisfaction, which can lead to resignations or absenteeism, because staff feel even less valued, due to an increased number of complaints and a 'why bother?' attitude. We have already acknowledged that a lot of these problems exist within our health services. We are back to the whole cycle again of tighter control and increased staff cynicism.

Are we at that level in our health service? I think today has shown that there are some people who are starting to feel we are at that level. I think it is important to note that people and quality processes make for a quality health service. A poor quality health service results from a poorly-designed and badly-operated process.

The question I would ask is do we have a place within the organisational structures for IT responsibilities – procedures, processes and resources for implementing quality management? Is there a solution? Well, I do not know. Is there a crisis? But do not blame the singer, if the song is written poorly. Instead, rewrite the song.

So what do we need? We need clear leadership. And we have been shown clear leadership in the form of the health strategy. This is a framework for delivering our health services into the future, and this document was developed following wide consultation throughout the service. In the strategy, the quality agenda was clearly brought to the front. It is stated very clearly that there is a need to embed quality into our daily activities. Quality is not an add-on – it is not something we can tag on at the end. It is part of the way we work.

But, if we want staff to take on board this new way of working, we have to show them that there are tangible benefits. What is in it for them? We have to work through our staff. We will possibly need structural changes. A quality approach ensures that time and effort is spent on the right things – it facilitates continual improvements and measurement of progress. It makes the effort visible to specification and measurement.

Quality is integral to patient care and does involve changes to process, structures, people and culture. Any quality service must place the patient centrally. So, I think we do need to make changes.

I would like to leave you with a final thought: Whether we have a crisis or not, we need to change our health services. Unless we do it ourselves, within acute services, our agenda will be forced.

X

EDUCATION & TRAINING FOR THE ACUTE SECTOR: PROCEDURES & PROCESS

PROFESSOR KEVIN O'MALLEY

CHIEF EXECUTIVE, ROYAL COLLEGE OF SURGEONS IN IRELAND

My perspective as a Chief Executive of the Royal College of Surgeons in Ireland is a perspective that has to do with quality training and the provision of quality healthcare. For many years, it was considered reasonable, certainly accepted, that our young medical graduates would travel abroad for the most – and, in some cases, for all – of their post-graduate training. Many never returned to this country.

It is generally accepted nowadays that this is no longer acceptable. First, we need our most recent graduates to contribute to our healthcare system in the context of their post-graduate training. It is realised that there is an over-dependence on overseas graduates in this regard. I think there would be a general view that we should be in a position to provide post-graduate training – in other words, to be self-sufficient in this regard.

In the past, Irish trainees left for two main reasons. The first was a perception that training in this jurisdiction was rather poor – and certainly there was poor training in many specialities. The other reason for immigration – permanent immigration – was the poor career prospects of such individuals.

All of us involved in post-graduate training nowadays – the surgical colleges for which I am a member, Professor Brian Keogh as Past President of the Royal College of Physicians, the various post-graduate faculties within these institutions, the Medical Council, the Department of Health & Children – and, indeed, all of our colleagues in the other colleges – have in a sense, woken up to the challenge implicit in providing quality specialist training.

One of the key events in this regard is the Register of Medical Specialists (RMS), which may not be familiar to all of you. This was provided for on the Medical Practitioners Act of 1978 but, in fact, was not implemented until four years ago. The RMS contains the names of those people who are judged to have trained to an appropriate level or, in the past, were appointed as specialists in their field of clinical activity. The idea here was, first, to inform the public of the specialist status of an individual and, second, to have a mechanism for informing other doctors of the specialist status of their peers. So, in a sense, the RMS is a very fundamental *quality assurance mechanism*. However, when you go back and look at how one gets on to the RMS, one becomes involved in *standards*.

If one takes the concept of the completion of structured post-graduate training, this involves the inspection of posts, the approval of posts, the development of training curricula, monitoring the trainers – a very complicated system that has to be applied right throughout the jurisdiction because of the disposition of hospitals and indeed of general practice. Such structures need transparency – there must be accountability – there must be adequate funding.

The Medical Council, on which I represent the Royal College of Surgeons, has set a number of aspirations for the next four years. One of these is that, by July 2003, all doctors in this jurisdiction will either be persons who have their name on the Register of Medical Specialists – in other words, they are specialists – or they will be doctors in training. The view would be that there really is no place, in practice, for any other type of person. It is realised that this is going to cause significant difficulties for certain groups of doctors. But, as an aspiration, I think it is a very reasonable one, because having one's name on the RMS is not mandatory. An addition to the RMS is the General Register, which is the primary Register, and of course anybody on that register is entitled to practice.

Putting together all the mechanisms involved in structures for specialists training costs a good deal of money. I would like to acknowledge the role of the Department of Health & Children, through the post-Graduate Dental & Medical Board in providing enhanced funding for the administration of higher training.

One of the indirect issues that needs to be addressed is that, if one is to provide structured training, consultants and general practitioners also need to be allocated time to provide that training. It is no longer satisfactory to regard training as a kind of an 'osmotic' process. Training must be an active process, in which the specialist trains the trainee in a *structured* way. This is going to take clinical time from consultants and general practitioners.

A second important issue, as far as my institution is concerned, is that we would like to know what the likely consultant numbers are going to be in the future, because it is on this figure that we base the number of trainees within each speciality: the number of trainees are based on the projected consultant vacancies so as to ensure that we train the consultants of the future in a fairly structured way. It is very important to know what future consultant numbers are to be because, if the Department and the Minister decide on certain numbers, they must realise that there is 'run time' of between five and eight years to train a specialist. It will take time to make up the deficit.

The next point I want to make is the concept that you can only have **quality training** where there is quality of healthcare. Quality of healthcare, in our view, requires a minimum 'critical mass' of trainers, of providers of health care: in other words, consultants, as well as a critical level of allied health care professionals and a minimum critical level of patient throughput.

This means that, for any reasonably sophisticated level of training, it is very difficult to provide it in the smaller hospitals that dot this country. This is an old political chestnut: it was proposed over 25 years ago that we should rationalise the number of hospitals and consolidate on a much smaller number of campuses. This, however, is a political 'hot potato' that has never been grasped and I do not expect it to happen in my time.

The last issue I want to raise briefly is that of revalidation: The notion that once you have your name on the RMS, it will not automatically stay there forever. One would have to show, to the satisfaction of the Medical Council, that one remains competent in one's speciality. This would probably be based on a number of different components, including Continuous Professional Development, peer view of practice, clinical competence and so on.

This is going to require legislative change and my understanding is that the 'writing is on the wall'. It would also require that specialist Registration be mandatory because, if it is voluntary, it will not work in my view.

So I conclude by saying that there is fair consensus on the way forward for specialist training. There is also a fair consensus on the main quality assurance issues, particularly in so far as doctors interact with patients within our healthcare system. This is, in fact, a very complicated area with major funding issues and, indeed, it has major legal implications.

XI

HIGHER MEDICAL TRAINING IN THE ACUTE
SECTOR: RECENT DEVELOPMENTS & KEY ISSUES

PROFESSOR BRIAN KEOGH
CONSULTANT PHYSICIAN
AND FORMER PRESIDENT, ROYAL COLLEGE OF PHYSICIANS

Much of what I have to say is complementary to what Professor O'Malley has said. But I do believe that it is important to really get the message over that what we are talking about is not aspirational and we have, with the co-operation of the Department of Health & Children, been able to bring about real change in the training programmes in this country since 1997/98.

Change is always very difficult to bring about. But we have been successful, as is evident from some of the numbers that are presently in training. I would also like to touch on some of the problems, as Kevin O'Malley has outlined them, that face us all in the process of providing trainees with experience over an extended period of time.

Just let me run briefly through a number of points that are relevant. There has, of course, been a long and valued system of informal medical training in Ireland. We all understand that. Irish medical clinical training has always been excellent – and recognised throughout the world – going back as far as the early part of the 19th century when this country had an extraordinary status in the training of doctors.

This training comprises registration, which is the ordinary intern year, which is supervised directly by the Medical Council and which is currently under review. There is about two or more years of general professional training, as an Senior House Officer (SHO) or as part of the US First/Second Year Resident, Education and Accreditation programme. Experience is gained and this allows the trainee to branch off into various disciplines – not only medicine but possibly surgery, general practice and public health. Intensive specialist training, in the old scheme of things, was related to four to six years, in which the trainee concentrated on the speciality which he or she intended to practice as an independent consultant.

Then there was the tradition of trainees spending some time abroad, either in the UK or North America, for the purposes of obtaining specialist training, or learning special skills to bring back to Ireland.

Now – hopefully – we can keep these people in Ireland because we have the skills, and we have the expertise, here. Professor O'Malley has already commented on the Medical Council and this is a very important aspect of the specialist training programme, particularly since relevant European Directives require us to have specialists registered in training in medicine.

Following discussions with the Department of Health & Children, we were able to finally gain support, not only in regard to the trainee programme, but also with regard to the young doctors who trained here at home. There was a considerable deficit of doctors – particularly at the periphery. It was obviously important that we were able to make up that balance and basically produce our own doctors and keep our own doctors at home and well trained. We worked very closely with the Department in recent years and, in every respect, we have invested effectively in this training and been accountable for the monies we have got from them.

In regard to structure and processes that are in place, and what actually happens within the framework of our training programme, it is very complex and very detailed. This is one of the reasons, of course, that our colleagues found the change process difficult but – for the trainer, and for the trainee, very important. The distinction between the difficulties with service, as distinct from those of the trainee, is because they deal with different issues. The situation, first, was such that we appointed a Dean of Paramedical Training to the College of Physicians. This appointment was funded by our programme with the Department. The Dean is responsible to the College for training and to the Irish Committee of Higher Medical Training (ICHMT).

These are the structures embedded in the training process. When somebody enters the training programme, first he/she has to have their membership of the RCP. He/she is usually qualified a minimum of three years. Once he/she gets into the programme, the following aspects of this training develop.

First, there is the development by the relevant national speciality body or society of a curriculum of training, describing the minimum duration, the content and the extent of training programmes for the speciality. So, we rely on the specialists and the specialist organisations to provide their training programme.

Second, there is the identification of a suitable Registrar post which will be filled – or capable of transition to a special Registrar post and thereby obtain training and education approval from the ICHMT. In other words, posts that were Registrar posts are inspected by the ICHMT and, if they are suitable for specialist training, then they are approved by the ICHMT.

Third, this process involves an annual competitive recruitment and selection process. We have provided for inspection, by a special panel on behalf of the ICHMT, of each post to ensure that it reaches the training and educational standards required – or can be brought up to these levels. In other words, we visit each hospital or department if they put in an application to have their post recognised for training and the post is inspected by members of the ICHMT to make sure that it is up to standard.

The development of a speciality-specific training record or a log book, to be maintained by each trainee as a record of the training obtained, brings in accountability. The trainer, and the trainee, review that log book every three months. Following this review, we also have an annual assessment by a speciality panel, attended by trainer, trainee and a review body, usually comprised of members of the ICHMT. Finally, there is a penultimate year assessment interview and we bring in an external examiner to make sure that the training has been on track – the trainer and trainee are interviewed and a decision is made whether the individual has satisfied the criteria laid down by the ICHMT.

There has to be, of course, an appeals mechanism and we have an appeal mechanism if the trainee is not happy with the trainer or if he/she is not happy with the hospital. They have an opportunity to appeal to the ICHMT and have their training reviewed.

The development of these structures and process required the recruitment of national specialist Directors to co-ordinate each training programme and its trainers and trainees, as well as the creation of an Executive Office within the College. That is what happens within each speciality. If it is a large speciality, we have a National Speciality Director, who monitors the performance of both the trainer and the trainees.

It has also been recognised that additional skills training must be provided on a regular basis. Accordingly, we have training for the trainers, especially appraisal assessment and interviewing for selection and, finally, management training for the Specialist Registrar.

If we take the current data (2000/20001), it underlines the problems of manpower down the road. In rehabilitation medicine, as you can see, there is just one trainee present there; in genital/urinary medicine, there are two and, in general internal medicine, there are seven. We were, in fact, hoping that there would be more in the last field – that is, pure internal medicine, because it is a critical part of the training process that we get enough individuals who are trained in both general internal medicine and the speciality we are talking about here – pure internal medicine.

Again, if you take dermatology – there are six in training at the moment and we expect six in the year 2001. There is one individual in research. We have four in palliative medicine, 15 in public health medicine, respiratory medicine – and on through the common specialities. The total involved in hospital medicine is 17 and there are 15 in urinary research outside the country.

We now have well over 252 trainees presently in the system and as you can imagine that may pose problems for us in the future.

CONCLUSIONS

My major concerns are twofold. First, that we will have to regulate the numbers coming into the training programme; it is very important that we do not take on too many, otherwise we may have problems at the far end. Second, it is critical that the manpower planning programme looks very carefully at this situation: we must be able to slot these trained individuals into the different specialities. It has been emphasised that the specialist training programme does not guarantee a consultant post as we know it in Ireland: but it does, in fact, give the individual a training that allows him/her to practice medicine if he/she is an Irish graduate, anywhere in Europe – or if he/she is a foreign graduate coming in as a specialist to Ireland, it gives them that particular benefit. Generally, we would find that a number of these individuals will automatically go away for a year or two – to get further training, as happened in the past, but only just for a year or two, which, in any event, I think most of them would wish to do.

So that is the current position. I would emphasise again that, in regard to medical manpower, the importance of the numbers coming in and that is vital as far as I am concerned. We must control the numbers coming in. We would seek help from the individual, those in the specialism and the Department of Health to know something about what the future holds for these individuals, so that we can do what is best for all of the stakeholders in the acute system.

XII

THE CENTRAL ROLE OF THE PRIMARY SECTOR IN REFERRING ACUTE HEALTHCARE IN IRELAND

DR MICHAEL BOLAND

DEAN OF POST-GRADUATE STUDIES,
IRISH COLLEGE OF GENERAL PRACTITIONERS

I am delighted to address the particular issue of integrating general practice into acute hospital care, in the context of fundamental reform. I believe that fundamental reform is really what is required and I am delighted that the public apparently seem to have some appetite for it, based on the BUPA Ireland/ESRI survey (2001).

I want to begin with the World Health Report. In its Introduction, it places the ultimate responsibility for healthcare with government. It is very important that, as we move to a private, possibly mixed private and public system, with a variety of providers, there is somebody that has ultimate responsibility.

The word 'stewardship' has been applied to this idea, and I believe that is the role for the Department of Health & Children in requiring them to have an oversight of the entire system. We need to be sure that as we move forward and make changes, that people do not fall out, and that we do not end up with the American situation of 40 million people without health cover. That is of great concern, I know, to family physician colleagues in the US – it is a real issue for them.

The Report makes the point that many countries are falling short in terms of their potential for health services, in terms of death and disability. It also notes the point that prepayment schemes can reduce 'out of pocket' expense, and, therefore, prepayment schemes – if you are operating in a public/private mix system – are the way to go, and that private and voluntary sectors, generally speaking, can be better used.

That may seem self-evident to you, but it was a fairly major statement from the WHO. So, hopefully, what we are looking at is a new partnership in health care, with the patient at the centre of it, with the healthcare system, medical practice, and as you have heard from my two colleagues, the medical education system all supporting the system and with government in the background with the 'stewardship' function.

So, we need to look at ourselves very carefully, and this is time for fundamental review. There is absolutely no upper limit to the amount of money you can spend on health care. So the fundamental issues are about the choices nations are prepared to make. It is about how much you want to spend on healthcare, rather than on education and roads and a whole lot of other options. We are by no means the lowest amongst our European partners. But if you look at public expenditure on health as a percentage of total public expenditure, we are in the middle again. In other words, we are making decisions about the proportion of our public expenditure that is going on health, which places that figure higher than other of our European partners.

So when you hear arguments in the health debate that we are not spending enough, be aware of the fact that this involves cutting into public expenditure on other things. There are opportunity costs in increasing our spend.

The other issue, allied to that, is the notion that we always compare ourselves in terms of number of specialists, or numbers of health workers, with other European countries. This is completely fallacious. We should make our own decisions as to what our proportions should be. I am sure I do not need to remind this audience that the proportion of spending on acute hospitals is 55% of total spending on health. That is a big slice and that figure has remained unchanged in the midst of the changing figures over the last 30 years or so.

The World Health Report has this statement:

> ... concern with demand is more characteristic of changes in the third generation [it was talking about the third generation of health reforms] currently under way in many countries, which includes such reforms as trying to make money follow the patient and shifting away from simply giving providers budgets, which in turn are often determined by supposed needs.

I think that is a fundamental statement about the nature of the health care reform that we may want to consider. We have heard a great deal of demands – about added spending on the supply side. More of this, and more of that, in order to deal with the waiting lists and so on. Very little consideration is given about how you moderate demand within a healthcare system, and how we actually undo the increased demand that has been a characteristic of the last 10 years. Unless we get hold of that, simply providing more money to meet the immediate urgent demands of the acute hospital sector, in particular for more spending on the supply side, will be a short-term solution. It will not get us out of the trouble we are in.

According to the WHO Report, people's expectations are greater than ever. There is a question about the need, as opposed to the demand: again, the WHO Report says:

> if services are to be provided for all, then not all services can be provided.

It may well be that in actually putting together our healthcare system, we may not be able to meet the demands of all the people. There have to be compromises, and somewhere along the line those compromises have to be made. I want to refer to the issue of Ethics. I think we need to talk a great deal about ethics as we get into any reform process about what the fundamental values in health care ought to be: Equity, quality, cost-effectiveness, certainty and relevance.

But we also need a humane system – one that deals with patients in a humane way. Sometimes we can get blinded, as medical professionals, in our attempts to come to terms with the technology, to that cardinal element of *care*. Also we need rationality. By that I mean that 'yes, let's have evidence-based medicine, let's look for good evidence – but even where we don't have evidence (and there are a lot of areas where we don't), let us at least behave rationally in terms of what we do know and not give ourselves carte blanche, as it were'. WHO has proposed this new universalism that basically looks at somewhere between basic simple care and everything medically useful, you have **essential** care. It definition is determined by cost-effectiveness. The question is whether this essential care going to be provided to the poor or to everyone. The new universalism would suggest that everyone gets essential care: that is the framework for a health service. That is a move away from classic universalism, where everybody got everything, and selective primary care, where only the poor get essential services, much as happens with our GMS.

So, within PMI, we have a really strange situation in this country in that, on the one hand, we have everybody entitled to 'free' hospital care and yet 40% of them are going out and buying a second health package. Some 25% of total health spending goes on private medical insurance, paid for by over 45% of the population, all of whom, as I say, are already eligible. The only reason they are doing it is to beat waiting lists, to get personal specialist care and to enjoy better facilities. Therefore it is not a true, comprehensive healthcare system in its present form. I believe that can change.

Let me refer to the legislation within which PMI operates. I said it before – I say it again – I have some concerns about the fact that community rating applies at the hospital level and not at the community level. It seems to me that, if you want to use primary care as a means to control demand (the 'gatekeeper' role), the last thing you should be doing is having no community rating at the primary level, because those people who should use the services may be deterred. Unless, of course, we intend to make public provision for all the patients at high-risk at the community level.

In relation to the ethical issue, I want to give you a quick piece of history in relation to general practice in this country. Prior to 1972, we had what was called the Dispensary system. This meant that there were two tiers of general practice care. Public patients were seen in the Dispensary, which was usually a pretty basic building, in the morning. There was no choice for patients, it was overcrowded, there were frequent complaints, and doctors were paid by salary. Later on in the day, private patients were seen in the House, where there was choice, comfort and the doctor was paid a fee per service. It was a system that was an ethical challenge, not only to the healthcare system, but also an ethical challenge to the individual doctors who operated it. There was only one reasonable thing to do – which was what happened: it was abolished.

I think the system that currently operates in the acute hospital system – where we have what is effectively the Dispensary system as applied to the hospital sector – needs to be abolished. It should be replaced by a system where you have providers of healthcare competing in an open market, and where access is there for patients of all categories.

We should be looking to a single service, with doctors on a single site, with choice for all: if you do this as part of the fundamental reform, you will have fewer complaints, and it is possible, within that context, not overnight, but eventually as a matter of strategic policy, to have multiple payers using mixed methods of payment.

We need to have some sort of partnership with people in relation to this. I am not going to go into this in detail, but I think the public are significantly misinformed in relation to healthcare and much of the demand which we are seeing at the level of general practice, and which translates itself into demands for MRI tests and all sort of other things, are based on essentially misinformation with the patients.

General practice can help to redress that – if they have the time and the incentive to do so. So we are in a situation of expanding demand for healthcare, and have been for the last 10 years. Increase in public demand for services, rising cost of technology and drugs, increase in employment costs, demographic changes, while on the medical side, there is more talk of accountability and more defensive medicine – a lot of which is fuelling the flames.

The only way we have to control the system, as it stands, is where people have access to the public hospital system by waiting lists, with poor facilities, impersonal service and even sometimes by the suspension of service. We seem to think that if we make it discouraging enough, some patients at least, especially if they do not really need to be there, will not be there.

This, I believe, is not working as a strategy to control demand. Many of you will have seen me show this particular illustration before. It is a picture – a triangle – of health care. You have health occupying most of the population, a good proportion of whom are in 'self' care. Substantial numbers are in primary care and less in secondary care and less again in tertiary care.

We have a referral system so that the control of the movement of patients from primary care into secondary care is between the GP and, on the other hand, the receiving specialists. It should be a principle of health care reform that no one should be in tertiary care who could be in the secondary; and no one should be in secondary care who should be in the primary cohort; and we should not be looking after people in primary care who could be looking after themselves, if they were sufficiently enabled to do so. I think that what has been happening has created dependency in patients, whereas the whole ethos of health should be to move them up out of it, enable them to get out of the system, do ourselves essentially out of a job.

Whether that is basically in conflict with the notion of private medical insurance is a question I will leave with you – it is an important question, where you are asking yourself who 'owns' the provider system, and what are their fundamental interests. If those fundamental interests are purely commercial then, maybe, we have a problem because the interest of a commercial service is to increase the number of people that can be drawn into the service, or believe themselves needing the service.

If we are to start and try to reverse the situation within the area where I have an interest, then we are moving from primary to secondary care. That can be done by *clinical guidelines, equivalent infrastructure and criteria for referral.*

It is amazing that, under the current system, most GPs refer – without any pre-agreed guideline as to who should be referred and who should not. It is a broad intuitive clinical judgement. It is important that we do not interfere too much with that, but it does need guidelines and those should be agreed between the referrer and the specialist who is receiving and, I believe, management ought also to be involved in that process.

There are some other challenges. We operate in a situation of information overload. It is becoming increasingly difficult for us within the College of GPs to provide GPs with all the information they need in a digestible form. Any of you who have gone on to medical sites on the Internet and looked for references will know that 14,000 is not an unusual number. Side by side with that – paradoxically – there is *implementation* delay. Because of this, important new information is not getting down to the point of application without serious delay. Patients, on the other hand, also have access to a great deal more information – and, unfortunately, a great deal more misinformation.

The other point to be made is this. The number of consultations in primary care is 18 million. The number of outpatient attendances in hospitals is about 2 million. About 4% of consultations are typically referred by a GP. You will see that it requires only a small shift in GP referral behaviour, in terms of the number of consultations, to reduce it from 96% of consultations dealt with by him or her down to 95%, and thus 25% fewer people reaching acute hospital care. Such is the nature of the interface that very small shifts in GP behaviour induce significant changes in the number of people reaching the specialist. It is not true to say that everyone who is in hospital needs to be there.

Patients often attend the hospital repeatedly for regular check ups because it reassures them. The clinician involved finds it reassuring to see that his intervention is still a success. They do not *need* to be there. That is the reality. I think that is particularly true in endocrine care, haematology, renal psychiatry and rehabilitation, where the percentage of returns of those clinics is over 90%.

The other point is that the evidence of referral rates between GPs shows substantial variation – up to a four-fold variation between GPs and the extent to which they use the referral option. That underlines what I said earlier.

What I am suggesting is that, in addition to the kind of general measures that I mentioned already we also need to do something with the budgeting. We have heard descriptions of how that operates within 'Managed Care'. I would suggest that we 'break out' of the sort of straight-jacket in which we find ourselves, where budgeting is either for primary care or for hospital programmes. We need to change that – to set up 'service budgets' that cross the boundaries, where care is really integrated because the money is integrated. Referral and investigation budgeting is something which could be operated in much the same way as has already happened in relation to indicative budgets for drugs. That has been quite successful.

Second, going on from what I said earlier, I believe that the ideal method of funding for doctors is to have one contract on the same site: you may have contracts with different purchasers, but **one** contract. That should be a mix of payment, capitation, fee per items and so on.

Part of the difficulty in acute hospital care is that some parts of it are salaried, which set up one set of incentives, and another part of it is largely procedure-driven, which sets up a completely different set of incentives. You can have multiple people funding it.

The other crucial step is to consider the idea of placing some portion of income at risk. That is a situation where 75% of the doctor's income is guaranteed and the remaining 25% varies according to performance.

Primary care 'teams' within a healthcare system is very important, and we are lucky in this country that we have an established clear difference between our generalists and our specialists.

The distinction of hospital-based care and community care has really disappeared. We now have a lot of specialists operating within the community setting .So we need to define who are the generalists. In our Irish system, I believe they are the GP, the practice nurse, the community nurse and perhaps, at some point in the future, the pharmacist, though I do not think we are yet ready for that. These people should be operating out of a common patient list, and a common patient record. There should be patient choice so that these teams may be chosen by the patient and the patient can move if they are not happy. It is those units that should form the basic 'building blocks' of the Health Service. They should be built up into areas that may share common out-of-hours arrangements, for example, and those wider elements should be built into a region. The notion of delivering services geographically at the primary level is one that I think we should consign to history.; For this to be successful we must also have a good electronic communication links between GPs where essentially they are co-ordinators of care, as well as deliverers, with all of the relevant agencies.

Finally, I want to say something about the whole notion of what is the potential demand out there, if we do nothing. We can envisage an illness like depression as a kind of iceberg. A GP sees about 75 new cases of depression a year. Broadly, 13 are referred, four are admitted. We know from general health questionnaires and other studies that have been done that there are 300 other people who meet the clinical criteria of depression out in the community. It is quite obvious that if they were all to turn up and look for care, the system would collapse, because these icebergs also exist in relation to, for example, upper respiratory infections, arthritis and a number of other conditions.

So the challenge for the health care system is not to provide care for all patients, *but to provide care for those who need it most*, because some of these patients with depression are actually coping with it and will not require our intervention. The crucial thing is that the ones we do have are the right ones, and that is not always easy.

Patients will not make our job easy in determining which of them need services most, but that is part of the challenge that we have got to face. So, in relation to health care, I believe that it is vital to know what are the limits, and what are the limits that we as a nation decide that we are going to set ourselves and not fool ourselves that we want to provide care for absolutely everybody.

In summary then, the key elements of reform that I am suggesting is that we invest in a primary care-led service, and that does require some investment; that we have access to secondary care through primary care as we have had; that we have an appropriate generalist/specialist balance. We have a situation where we have a good balance between the number of generalists and the number of specialists. If we now try – in the short-term – to try to solve our problems in the acute hospital sector by greatly increasing the number of specialists, we will upset that balance.

Barbara Starfield and a number of other international people have made it clear that the number of specialists you have within your system is one of the key indicators as to its cost. I also believe we should have multiple payers with a single contract – some portion of which is at risk, mixed funding that does not distort practice and integrated personal and community approach to care. We should have professional guidelines to determine particularly referrals which should be assessed, and any innovation in healthcare should be assessed, including demands for technology. We should maintain real choice for most of all levels and CPD.

So if we are looking to the future, we need to define what we want nationally, build our partnership with patients, develop greatly our emphasis on prevention and screening, effective teamwork and balance between primary and secondary care. We should have an accountable system and I believe that information technology in communication technology can transform our administration. Many of our worst features have to do with poor administration.

XIII

DEFECTING FROM THE MEDICAL PROFESSION: A PERSONAL PERSPECTIVE

DR RUTH DOWLING, MD, MBS[14]

Although I have just completed a Master of Business Studies programme here in the Smurfit School of Business, this was not always the road that I intended to find myself on. Just over a year ago, I started my Intern year after spending my six years training in medicine in Trinity College.

At the start of my intern year, I really felt like I was going to have a career in hospital medicine. That was what I was adamant that I wanted to do. But towards the end of the year, I came to the realisation that, not only did I think that I was not going to stay in hospital medicine, but I thought that perhaps medicine in any shape or form was not for me.

So I looked at my different options and I applied to do the MBS here in the School of Business. When I came in contact with Ray, he was interested in my story, in the sense of the manpower crisis that people are speaking about in the medical profession today.

Professor Keogh has said that there is a kind of crisis in regard to trying to reduce the numbers that we have on the Specialists Registrar. From my perspective, there is another crisis – one of *trying to keep people in the system, to reach the Specialists Registrar stage.*

I hope to offer two perspectives here today. The first is a purely **personal** perspective that I hope will give an (albeit perhaps limited) insight into what medical professionals may feel about the whole issue of students leaving medicine. More importantly, the second thing that I hope to offer you is other people's perspectives, other doctors' perspectives on the issue of leaving medicine.

You are probably wondering how I am going to do that. I will tell you: When I came to announcing to people that I was going to leave, I got quite strong 'knee-jerk', honest, from-the-heart reactions from doctors, at all levels, from interns all the way up to Consultants, about my decision. Yes, it was

---

[14]   Dr Dowling qualified in medicine and, on completion of her internship, took a principled and informed decision to leave medicine. She completed her MBS in the Smurfit Graduate School of Business with First Class Honours and is presently a Credit Analyst with Anglo-Irish Bank.

triggered by the fact that it was me that was leaving, but the reactions that came from doctors were really related to the subject of leaving medicine itself, as opposed to me personally. I am going to give you these very much anonymous reactions that I got from about 12 doctors, when I told them I was leaving, or they heard from other people that I was leaving. I am hoping that when you hear the perspectives of a wide range of doctors, you will get a broader insight into what a wider range of medical professionals may feel at the moment about this important issue.

I want to start, very briefly, by saying to you that I am aware that there are definitely some limitations to my personal account, which I am sure you are probably aware of yourselves. The first very obvious limitation is that this is very much a personal experience, as opposed to an evidence-based account, and I am aware of that.

The second thing is, of course, that this is the personal experience of someone who has left, so it is really up to you to decide whether perhaps this has biased me. I do, however, feel that I have some strength to offer in my account. The first is, as I outlined earlier, that I am actually going to give you the perspective of a few different people, and not just myself. In order for me not to contaminate my evaluation, when I give you these quoted remarks I am not going to comment on them, save for where I need to introduce them. I think you would lose the advantage of having other people's perspectives, if I were to give you my take on their perspectives. Then I think the second strength is that I also listed out the limitations. I think it is very much the personal experience of someone who has left the profession. Professor Kinsella had been on the phone to me six months ago and asked me to do this same presentation when I was still working in hospital. I do have to admit I would have found that difficult. But now I feel that I am free to say what I feel, but at the same time I have absolutely no agenda.

OTHER DOCTORS' PERSPECTIVE ON LEAVING THE MEDICAL PROFESSION

Firstly, the perspective from other people. I am going to take you from the level of an intern which I was, all the way up to the remarks of a consultant. This first remark is from a friend of mine – he heard through somebody else that I was leaving and we met later in the week, on a Friday night. This is what he said to me. He said, '*Ruth, rumour has it that you are deserting a sinking ship*'.

The second two comments are also from interns. They are something along the same lines. They said, '*I am staying in medicine, hoping that it will get better, which is probably naïve*'. The other said, '*I would like to leave, but I feel trapped*'.

The next three comments are from Registrars. A radiology Registrar said this to me, after I explained I was leaving: '*If I had my time back, I would probably do something along the lines that you are doing*'. Similar comments came from a GP-trainee, which I think is particularly significant in the sense that really, as you probably know, there is kind of an exodus out of hospital medicine now. There is a pattern towards moving toward general practice, in terms of young doctors in training. I think to be a GP-trainee is considered to be quite a coveted position. So I think this comment is particularly significant: *'I think you are probably right to leave'.*

The next three comments came from consultants. I suppose, in some ways, they have a slightly more paternal, or materialistic view on it, when they are speaking to someone like me who is quite young, or who was quite young in the profession. The first comment was *'I would not want my children to do medicine, there is no future in medicine'.*

The next comment requires an introduction. It was from a consultant, one of the few who asked me *why* I was leaving. I think that is quite a significant comment, because in fact very few consultants found the need to ask me why. The conversation came up, as it did many times as you can imagine during those few months. He said to me, *'Ruth, why are you leaving?'* and, I said earlier, quite honestly, I would not have felt as free to be quite as honest then, I said to him I could not see that I would want to work in this area long term. He replied: *'Most of us feel like that all of the time'.*

This last comment was from a lady consultant. I was at a wedding of a girl in my class – it was actually a husband and wife consultant couple. We were walking back down the aisle after the ceremony and she again asked me the question that I dreaded, as I felt different to everybody else in my class. She said *'What are your plans for next year?'* and I replied that I was actually going to the Smurfit School of Business to do an MBS – that I was actually leaving medicine. She turned to her husband and said, *'This wise young girl has decided to leave medicine'.*

I hope you are not sitting at the moment thinking that I have given you a very skewed set of comments. I have not given you all the comments of people who did not think along these lines. The only thing I can say to you is that I did get some comments from people, at all levels: particularly there were two consultants who really very strongly asked me whether I was absolutely crazy to leave the medical profession. I think it is important to say that.

The only reason I did not include them in my presentation is that I could not remember their exact words. Having said that, I really have to say that the overwhelming majority of the 'knee-jerk' reactions that I got from doctors were of the nature and tone that I just described to you.

I think really that a part of that was that, when I said to people that I was leaving – and I made the decision when I was quite young – that people in some way felt free to tell me how they really felt.

MY OWN PERSPECTIVE

So, shifting from the perspective of a few different doctors to my own perspective, I have to say that I am somewhat wary about this, not because I mind telling you, but because I feel like my own perspective probably gives only a limited insight into the medical profession. However, I will put my two pence worth in for what it is worth.

There were two reasons I left medicine, and I suppose I was trying to get this in a nutshell for today's presentation. The first reason is that you get this sense when you work in hospital medicine, that you are almost fighting a losing battle: you get this sense that all your efforts go into *not actually generating something positive, but maybe only eliminating a few of the negatives that are there.*

I am not saying that a lot cannot be done to actually improve the situation. I am not saying that. I am just saying how it felt for me. The point for me was that I really wanted to put my energy in a system, or into a career, that I felt would work *with* me and not that it was always constantly with the feeling that I was shouldering this under-funded service.

As I was thinking these thoughts, I was reading from one of my classes and I just came across this quote, quite by accident, and it summed up what I was trying to say. It was from the *Harvard Business Review in* January 1990. It says that

> ... *the hospitals function in spite of the system, only because of the enormous professional devotion of their staffs.*

For everyone who is still there, I do feel for them. I feel like they do their jobs in spite of the system, which is exactly why I left. I did not want to feel like I was working in a system that worked against me.

The second reason is really a bit more philosophical. People often bandy around this idea of 'Did you go into medicine for the right reasons?'. It is very hard to answer that question honestly about yourself. What I do feel is that I was quite happy to enter into the vocation that medicine should be, in the sense that I was perfectly prepared – and still am – to work hard. I was very committed to trying to achieve the best possible standards that I could possibly get for a patient. That was very high on my priority list. And I feel that is what the nature of the vocation of medicine involves, or should involve.

I thought when I started work that what makes medicine a vocation is not the nature of the work that I have described, but really the conditions of work that doctors are maybe forced to work in. For example, it is not hard work that is required of you, it goes way over the scale of hard work. It actually involves quite a lot of physical, and indeed mental, stamina to be able to work with the physical strain and the mental strains of these frustrations that I described earlier.

I have one parting thought. It is perhaps more relevant to the general population than it is to the people assembled in this room but it stems from the fact that really I think a lot of the general public feel that doctors have been complaining for so long, that their attitude has become 'what is wrong with them, there they go again, the doctors are complaining' – that type of thing.

For me, the lesson I took when I examined the health system with my own eyes – that I will take with me no matter what I do from hereon afterwards – is that, if you look at any group of individuals as they progress through a profession and find that they change, during that time, from being initially determined to overcome the problems in the profession, to gradually feeling defeated by these problems, then you have a problem.

If you look at junior doctors, as they progress from being a junior doctor to being senior doctors, and you see that consistently, year after year, decade after decade, or however far you want to go back, that you see that change – from a determination to defeat the system, to feeling defeated by the system – then I do think the onus is on people who are looking on to say what is wrong with their *situation*, as opposed to what is generally asked – which is what is wrong with *them*.

XIV

STRUCTURAL LEAKAGES IN THE IRISH ACUTE HEALTHCARE SYSTEM

RAY KINSELLA

**DIRECTOR, CENTRE FOR INSURANCE STUDIES,
GRADUATE SCHOOL OF BUSINESS, UNIVERSITY COLLEGE DUBLIN**

In the period since 1997, there has been an unprecedented rate of increase in exchequer spending on health. In his chapter, the Secretary General of the Department of Health and Children (DOHC) points to the significant increase in throughput within the system. More recently, he has pointed to an increase in hospital activity of 23% since 1997.[50] Equally, he notes the improvement of mortality and morbidity statistics.

Conversely, an international authority, Dr. David Store of the Harvard University School of Public Health, recently (2003) noted:

> *"Wards are shut; public health doctors are on strike; waiting lists and waiting times are larger, people are dying while in the queue and queue – jumping is not uncommon, while citizens have the longest life expectancy in the EU".*[51]

It is clear that "cutbacks" have already begun to take capacity out of the public system. New bed capacity, on the scale promised in the Health Strategy (2001), has not been provided.

Future demand for acute care will be shaped by a number of factors. First, there is a larger population, disproportionally represented along the eastern seaboard, a trend that is projected to continue. One of the most significant trends is the projected increase in the numbers of the elderly, who inevitably have a proportionally much higher usage of acute beds. This 'skews' the provision of acute care nationally and puts excessive pressure on facilities in the ERHA region. Some 11% of the population are elderly and account for over 40% of acute bed capacity.

---

[50] Secretary –General of the Department of Health and Children, speaking at the BUPA Ireland Health summit, Dublin, June 2003.

[51] *Ibid.*

Public expectations are a second factor and must be looked at in the context of an established right to travel within the EU in order to secure timely access to appropriate acute care.

There are also indications of changing epidemiological patterns that have important implications for acute as well as community care.

The Government's Health Reform Programme was introduced in June – October 2003. Let us assume that changes – both in institutional arrangements and in medical manpower – will happen. Let us also assume that the necessary Exchequer funding is available. Both of these, especially the latter, come close to heroic assumptions. Nonetheless, they allow us to raise this issue: while, in the post-1997 period, there is evidence of increased outcomes, there is a widespread belief that the increase was not commensurate with the scale of the investment (see Robbie Kelleher's chapter). The question is why? Are there any lessons for the conduct, and content, of future policy? A full explanation would require a detailed input/output analysis, which is beyond the scope of this present paper. Nonetheless, it is helpful to conceptualise the process of structural "leakages" in the Irish acute healthcare system.

A useful starting point is to differentiate between what may be called a "productivity" gap and an "output"/"outcomes" gap, which is the more widely-made criticism of the lack of impact of the doubling of healthcare expenditure between 1997 –2001.

In regard to a "productivity gap", a number of points may be made. The first is that the health services were chronically under-funded for so long – reflecting the "take out" of capacity in the 1980s and the cuts of the early 1990s – that that the increase in expenditure post-1997 was largely absorbed within a over-stretched, under-funded system that was merely playing "catch-up" with the additional funding. The structures, infrastructure (notably IT) and incentives necessary to transform additional expenditures into corresponding outputs were simply not there.

Central to this argument is that productivity in the services sector generally lags that of the manufacturing (particularly the high-tech composition of Ireland's internationally traded manufacturing sector) and is exacerbated by medical cost inflation, which is a multiple of consumer price inflation. Moreover, international studies by, for example, McKinsey indicate different productivity trends in acute health care between different countries, depending in part on the market structure/organisation. So part of the post 1997 phenomenon may reflect.

"OUTCOMES GAP"

We now address more directly the issue of why the "initial inputs" (a doubling of expenditure) do not translate into a corresponding "final outcome"

Figure 1 attempts to explain in a stylised form why this is happening, and what needs to be done about it. It also indicates some of the structural deficiencies that need to be addressed; all the more so given, on the one hand, increasing demand and, on the other hand, reduced availability of public expenditure. And it highlights the "Outcomes Gap" in acute healthcare between what *is*, and what *could be*, in a "Best of World" policy scenario.

FIGURE 1: STRUCTURAL LEAKAGES IN IRELAND'S ACUTE HEALTHCARE SYSTEM

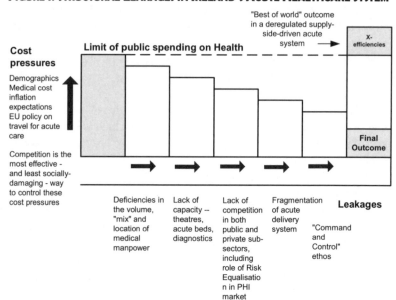

The first part of the diagram shows the money that goes into the system – about €10bn, of which, as a rule of thumb, about half goes into the acute system. Clearly, the scale of the "initial inputs" is not reflected in the "final outcome".

One way of attempting to visualise the dichotomy between, on the one hand, increased expenditure and, on the other hand, a disproportionally smaller set of outcomes, is to focus on "leakages" from the system. Across the bottom of the diagram are some of the "leakages". These reflect structural weaknesses, bad polices and a lack of competition-driven cost-effectiveness. These are the kind of "leakages" that have prevented public expenditure on health between 1997 and 2001 from being transformed into a corresponding improvement in health outcomes.

The first leakage is deficiencies in the volume, composition and location of medical manpower. The shortages – particularly with regard to consultants who drive the efficiency of the acute system – are addressed by the proposals in the Hanly Report (October 2003), which envisaged a more than doubling of consultant posts to some 3,600 by 2010. The point here is that, as consultant Colm Quigley, head of the IHCA, points out in his Chapter (IX), it takes at least 10 years to process/facilitate a consultant moving through the system. And the Government does not at present have the resources to commit to a long-term strategy on the necessary scale. Moreover (as McNamara and Fitzgerald point out, in their respective Chapters), teaching universities are already chronically underfunded.

The second "leakage" relates to capacity. Instead of the *additional* beds (particularly properly-serviced acute beds, which is much less than the published number of acute beds) that were promised in the Health Strategy of 2001, wards in some public hospitals are being closed. These cuts – when the Government's own Health Strategy highlighted the need for *additional* beds – represents a massive retrogressive step – and one apparently without any logic other than *ad-hocery*. Equally there is, by international norms, a shortage in theatre capacity. At the same time, the projected increases in consultant posts proposed in the Hanly Report will require additional capacity, as will the promised upgrading in the facilities of some of the local/regional hospitals. All of this would also be unnecessary or minimised within a system that was focussed on increasing private capacity in the interests of all, rather than on rationing demand in the public system.

Importantly, as Dr. Richard Brennan points out in his Chapter, there is a serious erosion in GP capacity as well as in distribution of GPs that is not aligned with social need – and not fully integrated with the acute system – even though GPs are the "gatekeepers" to the acute system.

In some nursing specialisms, such as midwifery, there is a critical situation developing in relation to entry and non-competition. Government initiatives in the field of nursing home care have not been sufficient to prevent serious supply-side strain. This raises serious issues not alone of the provision of care and over-dependence on overseas/agency nursing, there is an embedded clinical risk dimension.

The third leakage is a lack of competition – not alone in the private health insurance (PHI) sector, but as Professor Muiris Fitzgerald, Dean of UCD's Medical School, points out, also in the public system (see chapter VII).

The private – largely PHI-funded – sector is being suffocated because of a *dirigiste*, over-regulated system that is wholly at odds with the Government's official policy on competition,[15] within the wider services sector and in the economy generally. It is becoming increasingly difficult in this environment for

---

[15]   See, for example, *Towards Better Regulation*, Dublin, Dept. of An Taoiseach, 2003 (http://www.taoiseach.irlgov.ie/betterregulation).

private hospitals to remunerate capital (as Mark Moran points out in his Chapter), and yet there is compelling survey evidence[16] of the highly positive satisfaction ratings with the private sector right across the spectrum from the quality of healthcare to the quality of facilities. In other words, additional private capacity is urgently needed not alone to leverage capacity in the public system, but to help offset the socially-regressive cuts that are now taking place in our major public hospitals.

The religious nursing orders are beginning to move out and the opportunity cost of replacing their enormous personal and financial commitment is becoming increasingly evident. There is only a single new acute private hospital, developed in Galway, in the last 10 years.

RES AND THE "OUTCOMES GAP"

In this context, the implementation by Government, on 1 July 2003, after almost eight years' effort, of a manifestly unnecessary and disproportionate Risk Equalisation Scheme as part of the PHI regulatory system represents a tax on the customers of every potential health insurer coming into the State.

The "leakage" created by the introduction of an RES is fundamental to the capacity leakage. The anti-competitive impact is already evident in the fact that major global insurers, with the capacity to provide PHI cover, as well as long-term cover – which has not even begun to develop as a market and yet which is of key social and budgetary importance – are deterred from entry into the Irish market.

It is reasonable to assume that, in the period 1997 to 2001, at least three insurers probably would have entered the PHI (and, by extension, the long-term care) market. This represents a loss of value to the acute sector and more generally to the economy of some €1 to €2bn, because of a fatally-flawed regulatory regime and a lack of dynamic, supply-side policies to encourage private sector participation.

Tens of millions of investment in capacity-building as well as in expertise and new "business models" for Irish patients could have been brought in, at a whole range of levels in the acute sector four or five years ago. Now, these potential entrants have moved on into other opportunities. Capital is too scarce and balance sheets too strained to underwrite risks on the Irish PHI market getting its act together. In every other sector of the economy, Government looks to competition and deregulation and the private sector to deliver value – which means a more equitable and accessible acute healthcare system, except in private health insurance.

For potential insurance entrants, who could help take expenditure and risk off the public sector balance sheet and increase the total acute capacity, coming

---

[16]   *National Survey of Perceptions of Healthcare Service in the Public and Private Sectors*, Centre for Insurance Studies, ESRI/BUPA Ireland, Dublin, October 2000.

into Ireland's PMI "market" is not financially attractive. PHI regulatory policy is wholly at variance with the needs of the acute system. The negative effects of this are exacerbated by the prospective additional financial demands on the exchequer embedded in the Health Reform Programme.

The scope for moving expenditure – and risk – from the public on to the private sector's balance sheet is now slim. That is why the public acute system is simply unsustainable over the short to medium-term, in the absence of a fundamental shift in policy. And, under the existing system, there is still the need for major refurbishment and replacement of equipment for which budgetary provision, along the lines that is standard practice in the private sector.

RATIONALISATION OF DELIVERY OF A&E SERVICE

A fourth "leakage" is the fragmented system of delivering acute healthcare which existed in the post-1997 period and which is at the heart of the Government's 2003 Health Reform Programme. We have too many small "trophy" hospitals, replicating services and a central system of large public hospitals increasingly starved for funds; especially university teaching hospitals – another crisis in the making, since they are funding key teaching and research functions on a wholly inadequate basis.

A re-engineered three level "hub and spoke" system is needed – based on consultant-provided A&E services in national centres of excellence, supported by local/regional hospital and working with a series of networked GP clinics providing a wide range of sub-acute services. This would also help offset the national skewness in the provision of services, with referrals from areas outside of the ERHA area constituting, in some instances, some 40% of admissions to the acute system.

CHANGING THE POLICY PROCESS

A fifth "leakage" is embodied in a "Command and Control" ethic within the public and – through the long arm of policy – into the private sector. It is not clear that this issue is dealt with in the Health Reform Programme.

The process of reforming the system – the Health Reform Programme – is still "top down" instead of "bottom up". The net effect is a clogged-up "policy sclerosis"[17] that means the system is less informed, with less buy-in from stakeholders and more problematic negotiation process than would otherwise be the case.

An effective policy process can both address the "leakages" noted at the start and *also* ensure policy is informed by medical practitioners and service providers and developed in a "high trust" manner.

---

[17]   Sunday Business Post, "The Importance of Process in the Irish Acute Healthcare System", 23 June 2003.

Right down through the years, healthcare strategy has been driven from the top, as part of a political process. This is quite simply wrong. It was the Taoiseach, Bertie Ahern TD, who said at the launch of the Health Reform Programme, "we need to leave politics outside the hospital door"[18]. If there is a real desire to do this, if it is not just political rhetoric, it can be done.

All of the major medical/nursing colleges and other representative bodies should be required to develop a plan setting out how "Best of World" healthcare outcomes could be developed, within their specialism and across the system. Real consultation with members should be mandatory. Spend an hour talking to an experienced Sister and you will see why the input of ordinary members of the medical and nursing professions is mandatory. This means that the plan is both informed and has "buy-in" from the outset.

It should be costed by the Department of Finance and then passed on to an All-Party Dáil Committee, after a public consultation process in the form of a forum with the public, headed by three eminent personages of the calibre and background of, say, former Central Bank Governor Maurice O'Connell, Sr. Consilio, who has been a campaigner for almost 40 years for those suffering from alcohol and drug abuse, both of which are at the heart of societal illness / dysfunction today, and the Department of Health and Children.

The All-Party committee should, after due consideration, pass the strategy for a reformed and sustainable "Best of World" acute healthcare system on to Government. This would really keep "politics outside of the hospital door".

The current institutional reforms are likely to increase "Command and Control", at a time when it is widely recognised that this approach is not just redundant in terms of "business models" and processes: it is absorbing resources, diverting the focus of the medical professions and destroying morale.

Unfortunately, as yet there is no integrated alternative vision of what our acute healthcare system could be because the different colleges and representative bodies have failed to bring forward, as a group, an "alternative" vision of what is possible.

Equally, the absence of any serious debate within the political arena which would focus on mitigating the "command and control" approach and, in particular, which would boost the private sector's part of the public/private mix – in the interests of the *total* capacity of the system, which is what equality and access is all about – is a cause for concern.

There are also very significant cost leakages from not allowing the internal dynamic of the market to operate. The cost of pharmaceuticals and major capital equipment, to take just two examples, are significantly cheaper in other EU countries. This is something wholly within the Government's control and which could materially reduce the "leakages", thereby freeing up resources for use elsewhere in the system.

---

[18]   On the occasion of the launch of the Health Reform Programme, June 2003.

Similarly, we are in danger of developing an "expectations"- instead of a "needs"-driven prescription process. A more rigorous approach than simply increasing the minimum prescription charge – which rose from €40 to €70 last year – is needed.

Equally, and perhaps more controversially, there are serious issues to be raised regarding the use of DRG-based case-mix as a means of allocating a hospital's budget. The issue here is *not* that hospitals with a more complex case-mix should not get a correspondingly larger allocation. Of course they should. It is simply the fact that a hospital may over-spend, despite intense surveillance by the Department, for all kinds of reasons other than an assumed lack of budgetary discipline.

By and large, the quality of financial control has been strengthened very significantly (to its credit, by Government investment) in recent years and is at least on a par with that of Government Departments and Health Boards. In these circumstances, the idea that taking a few million euro from one hospital (which though small in absolute terms, may be of enormous importance at the margin – for example, expenditure on a children's ward) and reallocating it to another hospital is fundamentally flawed; the impact of the reduction in the allocation to the hospital will – quite simply and inevitably – have to be borne by patients.

CONCLUSION

There are other leakages. But the point is clear, there is a "productivity gap" and there is a series of leakages arising from structural flaws in the system. By the time the expenditures flow through the system, there are so many leakages that the outcomes are greatly reduced compared with what they should be – and an even smaller fraction of what they could be, in a "Best of World" acute care model, incorporating x-efficiencies. We need a supply-side revolution to address these weaknesses while, at the same time, minimising upward "cost pressures" that threaten to subvert the Health Reform Programme.

XV

THE IMPACT OF CUT-BACKS ON ACUTE INTENSIVE HOSPITAL SERVICES: SOME PERSONAL REFLECTIONS ON NEW MANAGEMENT & ALTERNATIVE MODELS

DR DAVID HICKEY

CONSULTANT UROLOGIST & HEAD OF THE TRANSPLANT UNIT, BEAUMONT HOSPITAL

I just want to give an overview – I think I am reflecting the views of an awful lot of people at the coalface. I am going to go through what I think the real problems are.

We can start out with this story about George Best, which is not a bad metaphor for where we are in health. George is reputed to have been in the Clarence Hotel in the mid-1970s, having left Man Utd and having won £40,000 at the races at Epsom that day. He rang down for room service. He was dating Miss World at the time and was having a very high-flying life. Half an hour later, the door was gently opened and this fellow with the tails and the hat that these guys wear walked in. He looked at the room. Miss World was there in bed. George was in his silk underwear. Buckets of champagne, half empty, half drunk. Hundred dollar bills around the place. This little small wizened guy looked around, and says, *'George, where did it all go wrong?'*.

I think to some extent that might help tell us where we are in our healthcare service, except we might say, even more unkindly, did we ever have it right? We've had 10 years of unparalleled financial success. And this (**Slide 1**) is what we have been left with at the end of it. We are the third richest country in Europe; yet 28% of our children live below the poverty line – that is worse than New York City. We have the lowest social spending in Europe – 16% versus an average of 27%. We have an enormous number of people in prison – higher even, believe it or not, than Turkey. We have 8,000 people homeless currently in Dublin city.

As the aspirations of some of our politicians have been in the past, we are certainly far closer to Boston – in fact we are more like Boston than Boston itself – than we are to Berlin. I think that is the wrong emphasis for us.

SLIDE 1:

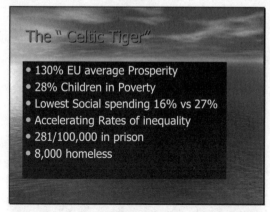

SLIDE 2:

Health Spending % GDP	
• USA	12.9
• Switz	10.6
• France	9.3
• Holland	8.7
• Belgium	8.6
• Ireland	6.8

We spend the lowest – about 80% of the EU average – on healthcare (**Slide 2**). We have the lowest number of doctors in Europe (**Slide 3**). When you look at the world, two countries where the situation is significantly worse than here – Pakistan and India – are the countries where our own Department of Health and Children is "stealing" doctors, bringing them to training programmes in Ireland. We have become a neo-colonial power, "stealing" these very scarce resources from countries less well-off than us. I read that at least half a billion dollars worth of medical education is stolen by the Western Europeans and Americans every year from third world countries. *That* is the way we have patched up our medical service over the last 10 years.

In terms of beds, we are at the bottom of the bottom rung. Spain is next worse above us and has 30% more beds per 1,000 of the population than we have – 3.1 beds per 1,000 of the population. So, in terms of infrastructure, in terms of cutbacks, you cannot conceive of cutbacks under these circumstances.

We have the lowest number of personnel, the least amount being spent, and the lowest number of beds in the developed world.

SLIDE 3:

Just to give you an idea of what Beaumont is like (**Slide 4**). Like all acute hospitals in Dublin, we are emergency-driven: 70% of the admissions to the hospital in 2001 were emergencies – either direct transfers on a Friday afternoon from the regional hospitals, or admissions from our own emergency room. We run at at 90% to 100% – often 115% – of capacity. We have had up to 35 stretchers in casualty at Beaumont Hospital at certain times of the year. So, we often run above 100% occupancy.

Now, as a model of healthcare excellence, France has 75% bed occupancy – this is felt to be around the ideal occupancy of beds in order to plan for an acute, an emergency and a general elective medical surgical service.

SLIDE 4:

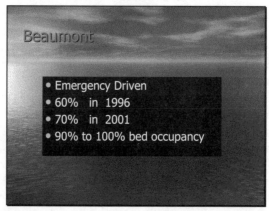

If you just take our own transplant centre, we are actually the biggest organ and kidney transplant centre within the UK Transplant Service (UKTS). In terms of numbers, we have now carried out close to 3,000 transplants, making us one of the largest in the world. We are the only pancreas transplant centre in the whole of Ireland, having patients referred down from Belfast for treatment in the Republic of Ireland.

SLIDE 5:

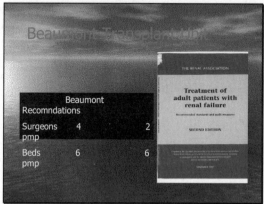

But this **(Slide 5)** is the reality of our situation in Beaumont. The red tattered document on the slide is one that I have pulled out four times over the past four years to write a report ... I have done four reports for Department officials on the dire straits in which transplantation finds itself in Ireland today. This is a 1997 report, and these are minimum recommendations from the UKTS -- minimum standards, by no means the ultimate at which we should be aiming.

Anyway, just to use these guidelines, we have four surgeons involved in kidney transplantation at Beaumont. We should have two per million of the population – eight surgeons. We should have six beds per million of the population. Now the problem with the transplant unit in Beaumont is like everything in the Irish healthcare service. It was built on an *ad hoc* basis. One particular surgeon went to the meeting, saw the technique, brought it back in the 1960s, people who liked him worked with him, he got a lot of publicity when he started. It was built totally on voluntarism. There was never a structure put in place. Then the thing became indispensable, and people could not get time off. Eventually, the thing just struggled along and, to this day, it is being run on that kind of *ad hoc* basis.

Now, we talk about people coming in and doing studies. We have had this accreditation stuff forced on us in Beaumont this year. I had some whiz kid from Harvard, or some place in Canada, come in and grill me. And I showed him these figures and I said, 'You know, good clinical practice? This is not safe – we have people lying almost in the same beds.' But they accredited the hospital.

And there was no ripple even – so I do not know whether that report, or any of the other reports sponsored by healthcare board managers, have the same validity. But I know certainly that, if accreditation meant anything, our transplant unit should have been closed down on the basis of those figures alone.

What also happened – and this is even worse in the current cutback situation – is that we have 30 beds in that ward. Six are for transplant, the rest for urology. On average, we have 15 transplant patients, which is the number those figures would suggest. This means that elective urology *never* gets in to Beaumont Hospital. So, if your grandfather needs a TR or a prostrate, he can forget it. If he has cancer, he has a good chance of being cancelled only once or twice – but he still cannot be guaranteed treatment. I had to cancel a radical prostrate on a 58-year-old this week. Now, think in terms of a man who is told he has cancer, is told he needs an operation, who has organised his entire life around coming into hospital, taking holiday, his wife getting the time off – and to have the whole thing cancelled on a Sunday evening because we had an urgent transplant and his bed was gone.

SLIDE 6:

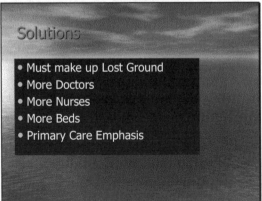

So, we are not doing very well by any of these parameters. The big thing is lost ground. We have never even been at the races, in terms of provision of facilities for healthcare. People are running out of the healthcare service now, because the facilities are so bad. I have a few pictures later on that I will show you of Beaumont Hospital – which is probably representative of other hospitals. The conditions for junior hospital doctors, the rooms in which they sleep, the kitchen in which they eat – I think people have no concept of the third world squalor in which these people have to live.

We need more doctors to even come close to the ideal European levels. We need more nurses – nurses are running out of nursing, again for the same reasons. Abuse, lack of facilities and the sort of 'matron and holy nun' concept that these people are on some sort of religious trip and do not mind working for nothing for incredible hours. That has been, yet again, this voluntarism that has been used and abused to the detriment of the system.

Another area where nurses are running out of is via internal promotion to kind of economic slots. Slots of suits, rather than nursing uniforms. Walking around with clipboards. In my own ward, where we have nurses barely trained, some of them go to Australia, some of them go to drug companies – and you cannot do anything about that. But you have the hospital itself recruiting people into these bullshit posts that are just duplicating and duplicating stuff all the time. This makes absolutely no sense to me. The situation is so bad for these people that they are just giving up.

SLIDE 7:

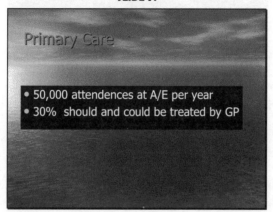

We obviously need more beds. But primary care is something we really have to look at. One of my big concerns is primary care – I think it could make a huge difference. We have about 50,000 emergency room admissions or attendances every year in Beaumont Hospital. Perhaps up to 30% of them could be treated by a GP if he had the time, the interest and the facilities. That is where in the future we must develop hugely our healthcare system.

Cuba, to my mind, has an exemplary Value for Money healthcare system (Slide 8). It has been visited by the BMA, the Canadian Medical Association, the Brazilian Healthcare Association. Yet there has never been a medical delegation from Ireland to go and look at Cuba's system – which has been eminently successful.

They have four levels of healthcare provision. The bottom two levels are incredibly important. They have this school at the bottom, the *bueno* for grandparents. This is a day centre where there is a doctor, a nurse, an epidemiologist, a gymnast, a dance teacher, a music teacher, there is even a guy who shows them how to play Ludo. They go down there for a couple of hours a day, play their games, do whatever they can. When they come out of hospital, they are met by these people and looked after. It is a sort of home away from home and a very wonderful social event for these people.

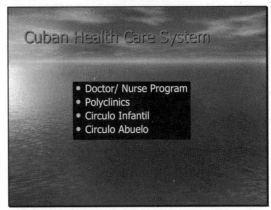

At the other end of the spectrum is a sort of crèche, for babies of six months and up. There is a paediatrician, or a person trained in paediatric medicine, in that crèche as well.

The main drivers of their system, however, are their doctor/nurse programme, and their polyclinics.

They have a doctor or a nurse now for every 120 families in Cuba. That means a doctor for every 400 patients, which is by far the highest in the world. There is a doctor on every street corner essentially. They have 460 polyclinics around the country – these are clinics in areas of population where minor procedures, chest x-rays, ECGs, suturing, minor fractures and that sort of thing are taken care of.

Also, what I think is a very useful innovation, is that the consultants from the really big centres visit these places on a monthly basis. The respiratory guy goes down, the neurologist goes down – and this saves the patient travelling. Most – 90% – of our admissions to outpatients in Beaumont are pat-on-the-back sort of problems – where the guy does not have a problem but they come down from Donegal, they wait for five hours, they get a slap on the back after a five-minute rectal examination or whatever, and they go back home.

I think this is a wonderful situation for the people of Cuba. And this is what Cuba has achieved over the past 45 years (**Slide 9**). Their number of doctors has increased from 6,000 to 65,000. The number of hospitals in Cuba has increased from 56 to 281. Their infant mortality rate has been reduced from 60 to 6.4 – which is just about the same as Dublin city today, and significantly better than Washington DC and most of the big US inner cities. Life expectancy has improved from 60 to 73 years and, finally, these people have developed the Latin American School of Medicine, where there are 5,000 students from the

Caribbean, Latin America and the State of Mississippi. These people are given a totally free medical education.

SLIDE 9:

	1958	2001
Doctors	6000	65,000
Hospitals	56	281
IMR	60	6.4
Lif Ex	60	73
Vac Rate	?	100%
Latin American School of Medicine		

Cuban Health achievements

Cuba has currently 1,700 doctors working around the world in third world countries. Now, we are stuck – Ireland is going in reverse. This used to be Ireland's role in the world in healthcare. But we are stealing from these people now.

SLIDE 10:

Cuba 45 years of Progress

Slide 10 illustrates the extent of what has happened in Cuba over the past 45 years. On the left is a very famous picture, taken by a guy called Corda. This is a small girl on the streets of Havana in 1958 with a wooden doll in her arms – a piece of wood with a little dress on it. On the right-hand side, you can see happy schoolchildren today, going to school.

If there was a just world, the man who designed this system would be getting a Nobel Prize for Economics, Peace – and Medicine as well.

But to get back to our own problems here in Ireland – we need buildings and we need beds. This again has been shrouded in layers and layers of bureaucracy. **Slide 11** shows the main entrance to the Pancreas and Neurosurgical Centre in Ireland – the biggest such centre in the country. That is Beaumont Hospital on the left. On the right, we have a sub-section of the Eastern Health Board, called the Northern Area Health Board. Now, the picture does not do this building justice, because there are waterfalls, and picnic areas out here as well on the right-hand side.

SLIDE 11:

SLIDE 12:

Again in **Slide 12**, this is the hospital here on the left-hand side! There are patients in there being treated. And on the right-hand side, you can see the inside of the Northern Area section of the Health Board – there are no people around there, there are lots of offices but nobody around at all. But there is a huge space.

And, finally – and this should go into some kind of photography competition – **Slide 13** shows the psychiatric unit at Beaumont Hospital, where you would imagine the environment would be designed to make you feel good about yourself and that you are a valuable member of society. That is the entrance to our psychiatric unit on the left. On the other side, again we have the Northern Area building in the Business Park in Swords.

SLIDE 13:

I think, personally, looking at things from the inside, that once you get in, you are going to get very well taken care of. I think we have fantastic doctors here in Ireland. I think Beaumont could be transposed to the Harvard Medical Center, and it would be a seamless transition. 90% of the guys working in that place have worked and trained in the United States and could make an absolutely seamless transfer. But the facilities – the pictures I have shown you of Beaumont are not extraordinary. I am sure hospitals, the older ones anyway, are in similar straits. Our hospital is not even 25 years old. The roof is falling off it, so there has been a €17m grant to patch that up with blue stuff. The windows are falling out, which costs another €5m or €6m – and wards are being closed to pay for this. This is a hospital that only opened in 1987.

But this is nothing to what is coming down the road **(Slide 14)**. 11% of our population at the moment are over 60. That is going to increase by nearly 40% over the next 10 years and, as we all know, that group of people take up over 70% of our healthcare budget at the moment. Diabetes – currently 4% of our population have diabetes, and another 4% have it and nobody knows about it. So, if people did blood sugars or urine sugars more often, it would double the number of diabetics being taken care of. By the year 2020 – these are WHO projections – 20% of the population are going to have diabetes. Ireland is the only country that has signed up to the St. Vincent's Declaration without living up to any of its aspirations.

SLIDE 14:

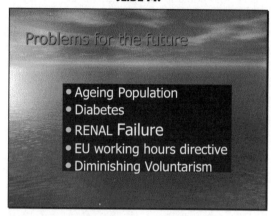

In terms of renal failure, we dialyse half what the Czech Republic does. Patients are not getting into GP's offices because of that. If that changes overnight, our services would be overwhelmed. We diagnose 60 patients per million of the population. The Czech Republic do 100, the United States do 150, the Italians do 200. We are moving into the third world, if we are talking about these figures. If the system fails, it is going to be a disaster for the patients.

There is a very interesting article on this topic in the *British Journal of Neurosurgery* by Walton, where he looked at the implications of the EU 58-hour working week directive for NCHDs. Astronomical – and soon it is going to be 48 hours. That is going to require a quadrupling of people, or so these people estimate. They are going to be able to work 58 hours a week – 6 hours of which must be freed up for educational and recreational purposes, and they have to have an 11-hour rest period after every 24-hour period of being on-call.

If you ask any of our NCHDs, you will learn that they are actually going to need to triple or quadruple the numbers in order to fulfil the 58-hour requirement.

Finally, people have had it up to the neck of carrying the can, struggling on, with lousy facilities, no help from the people who are supposed to be providing leadership in terms of Department of Health and Children. That is a thing of the past – the nuns are gone out of medicine. The old consultants who could threaten and bully their younger colleagues into working astronomical hours – that is gone. You are only going to get from medics and from nurses what you pay for them in the future – and we see that happening already.

We need huge increases in these two areas. How do we do it? My belief is that we have got to take politicians out of healthcare. I look at developments in healthcare over the last 20 years and I see a hospital in Cavan, and I know who was Minister for Health and Children during that period. You can actually do this like rings on a tree, or layers on a pyramid. You can go down to Limerick, it is the same thing; equally, in Tullamore, Naas and so on. And that has been the way healthcare planning, as far as I can see, has gone on.

I believe that what we need is a central development authority, based on people like yourselves, economists, doctors, nurses, technical people from the hospitals, representatives from the community. No politicians. We do need this authority to go and close the hospitals that are not viable. Again, as we mentioned earlier on, what we need are big hospitals, with motorways and 20 miles between them. For reasons best known to local politicians, these local hospitals are being kept open. We all know why they are being kept open – it is nothing to do with healthcare.

How are these things being financed? Again, this is not my area of expertise – but I do know that we need to build a new transplant unit for Beaumont Hospital, because it is no longer acceptable to treat people in the situation we are in. We need a hospital for renal failure and diabetes that can take 60 beds. We need to build that. How do we go about doing that? I am hoping to get some good ideas from the audience here today.

Perhaps the Public/Private Partnership concept is something that could work here. I would have no ideological problems with that – the government does not seem to have any money any more, so it has to come from somewhere.

Working in Beaumont Hospital today, I see it is in a crisis situation. The hospital is leaking, the hospital is cold, there is no air conditioning – nothing seems to be working well. This is probably a complaint everyone is used to hearing about, but it is literally at the stage where the place is in big trouble.

SLIDE 15:

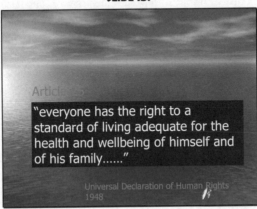

Finally, **Slide 15** shows Article 25 of the Universal Declaration of Human Rights, which we signed up to in 1948. As far as a significant proportion of our population are concerned, we are in default of our commitments to our citizens.

XVI

EXPANDING THE PRIVATE SECTOR: A NEW GENERATION OF PRIVATELY-FUNDED HOSPITALS FOR IRELAND?

MARK MORAN
CHIEF EXECUTIVE, MATER PRIVATE HOSPITAL

By way of a brief introduction, I would like to discuss customers. There seems to be a resistance when it comes to the word 'customers' when it comes to hospitals, which is something cultural that I think needs to change. I will give an overview of the private hospital system's contribution to the overall hospital system. The private hospital environment – what kind of environment are we operating in? Then I will turn to the key issues – the drivers of change and what, potentially, the future might look like.

So, by way of introduction, first, nominally at any rate, the Department of Health and Children does have a strategy committed to the public/ private mix. And we do have a mix of public and private healthcare. The issues of access and equity are very important – I like to think that when we talk about inequity of access – and there is an inequity of access right now – too many people focus on, if you like, dragging the private sector back to where the public sector is, instead of focussing on sorting out the public sector. I think when we talk about inequity of access, people should be less forgiving of the poor access that there is to the public system, rather than slagging off the good access there is to the private system, because that lets the whole system off the hook.

We operate in a system whereby acute healthcare is considered a right. Nominally, certainly in law, it is supposed to be a right, but in reality it is not getting delivered. We have heard numerous examples already today. Having said that, when we talk about private healthcare being privileged, 45% of the population are insured – 41% with VHI and there are other providers as well. The private hospitals, until recently, have been run by the religious orders on a not-for-profit basis, and the whole falling-off of voluntarism is an issue for the future, and definitely there are major cultural changes coming.

CUSTOMERS

I want to talk about our customers. Obviously the central customer of the private hospital is the patient, because ultimately that is the person to whom you are delivering the service. But from a private hospital management perspective, there are also a number of other constituents whom we have to serve. If you look at the bottom right-hand corner of a triangle, there is the consultant who operates in the hospital. Those consultants are a key, integral part of the delivery of service to the patient. They are not employees of the Mater Hospital – they are private, independent practitioners who have separate funding arrangements directly with the insurers. In effect, they have no financial arrangement at all with the private hospital. And they are a customer of the private hospital from the perspective that we do actually need to provide them with facilities. We need them to be able to provide care to patients.

The second group are the insurers and the Department of Health and Children, and anybody else who pays. 99% of the time the patient does not pay directly for themselves, their insurer pays or, in the case of the National Treatment Purchase Fund, it is the Department; or in the case of other insurers, there are other contracts, there are other sources. So they also are a customer, even though they are not a recipient of the service.

The third is one we have thought little of, although primary care is frequently mentioned – it also is a customer of the private hospital. We are, if you like, their conduit to appropriate secondary or tertiary treatment for their patients. The GP is presented with a patient problem, wants the patient to be seen by a consultant or ultimately operated on – or, in the case of medical patients, further diagnosed and appropriate medicine or treatment recommended. So, if you like, we have this triangle of customers but ultimately the patient is the central one, and always will be.

I just needed to point out that there are different constituents. It is not like a Ryanair situation, whereby anybody can decide where they want to go, and there is transparency in the price. It is a complex system here, whereby you have the referring doctor deciding what consultant he/she wants to refer his/her patient to. You have the consultant who, in many cases, operates in a number of hospitals, looking for access to the private hospital's capacity, and you have an insurer, or the Department or whoever – some third party payer – who is looking to get the service delivered as cheaply as possible, subject to quality constraints. And, in the middle of all of that, there is the patient who simply wants their problem solved, and hopefully at minimal cost to themselves.

THE PRIVATE HOSPITAL SYSTEM

What is the private hospital's contribution to the overall system? I will go back to reason the Mater Private was built in 1986, by the Sisters of Mercy. One of their primary considerations was to attract good quality consultants to work in the Mater Public. It was felt that, if there was a high quality private hospital on campus with the public hospital, it would be easier to attract doctors back from the leading centres – the Mayo Clinic, the Cleveland Clinic, John Hopkins in the States and various leading centres in the UK and Europe as well. It would be much easier to attract them back to a public job, if they had access to good quality private facilities where they could enhance their income but also practise in an appropriate setting.

We have increasingly seen over a number of years that the private sector has actually taken the lead in the introduction of new techniques and procedures. It cannot do so in areas such as transplant, but it can in areas such as diagnostic techniques. The first MRI scanner in the country was brought in 1987 to the Mater Private. A PET scanner is now in the southside of the city in a private facility. The first minimally invasive heart bypass was carried out in the Mater Private. So, we tend to be, I will not say world leading-edge, but certainly advances in technology have become accepted in the US and in Europe that pretty much tend to be very expensive. The private sector tends to take the lead relative to the public sector here, in Ireland.

We do have substantial capacity – and I will give you some comparative figures later. Mostly, non-commercial return on capital, because mostly all the private hospitals have been built and owned by the religious congregations. That is changing. We will have a look at that later. If the private facility is on campus, it promotes efficient use of the consultant's time because it means that the consultant, instead of having to leave the position of his public appointment to carry out his private work, can do it all on the one campus. Just to give an overview of our contribution to capacity – there are about 2,500 private hospital beds, with approximately 12,000 public hospital beds. The number is shifting a lot, particularly with the new health strategy. But of the 12,000 public hospital beds, 2,500 of those are designated private. So, in principle, 50% of private provision takes place in public hospitals.

You have seen already that the Department of Health and Children Acute Capacity Review has identified the need for 3,000 additional beds. However, it is interesting that the Department has no plans at present to engage in any public/private partnerships for the provision of those beds, although there is a strong feeling that central control of the acute system is absolutely essential going forward. I think that is a questionable stance, to say the least.

I want to talk a little bit about the private hospital environment. I am going to talk about four things: hospital funding, the insurance market, the critical issue of risk transfer, and competition.

The private hospitals' sources of income largely come from the insurers and, to be honest, VHI dominates that very significantly. So, typically, 80% to 90% of private hospital income comes from the insurer, and it is usually capped. So despite what people might think, the *modus operandi* of budgeting in private hospitals is fairly similar to that in public hospitals. VHI has such a dominant position in the market that every private hospital in this country has a maximum budget allocation per year, and if you happen to carry out more activity over the unit cost you have agreed, then it is tough luck, you have hit your cash limit.

Outpatient services whereby the patient has an entitlement to recover from the insurer subject to annual deductibles is, if you like, a non-contract income for the private hospital, and then you have varying degrees of much smaller numbers of self-paying patients, typically for non-insured treatments such as cosmetic surgery, eye-laser correction – there are a number of things that are excluded from insurance coverage. We also have public contracts and these are likely to increase with the National Treatment Purchase Fund but there are never going to be significant numbers here unless something substantial changes policy-wise.

Overall hospital funding – just to put the private sector into perspective comparatively with the public sector – the Department of Health spending on general and acute hospitals in 2001 was €3.2bn. That excludes the ambulance services; it excludes practically all non-hospital spending in the Department of Health and Children. The total private medical insurance for 2001 was €580m, of which approximately €123m went to the public hospitals, €145m went to consultants for professional fees and to private hospitals €312m. So, the private hospital budget is approximately 10% of the Department of Health acute and general hospital budget.

The PMI market is community-rated, we all know that. VHI is totally dominant with market share of 83% and BUPA Ireland, Gardaí, ESB and the prison officers make up the rest. BUPA Ireland is making significant inroads and hold around 10% to 12% of the market at the moment, having grown from nothing three or four years ago. But the insurance is totally focussed on hospital products, although there is increasingly a little focus on alternative medicine and some primary care but predominantly it is a hospital-based product. The claims cost, as I said was a total of €580m, equivalent to 8% of the Department's total expenditure or 18% of hospital expenditure.

Risk transfer is a critical issue and I think this is the issue that is going to determine whether there is a future for private hospitals in this country or not – or certainly whether there is going to be any expansion of the private hospital sector. Without going into details of risk equalisation, there are mechanisms of transferring risk at the moment. Here in Ireland, the private medical insurance market right now is not an insurance market. It is actually a claims/settling market – a claims/ settling operation. There is no insurance in the real meaning of insurance because risk does not really exist for the insurer. I am talking about pricing – the hospitals at the moment, the all-in rates that are paid to hospitals by VHI include issues like marginal rates and budget caps, so if there is more activity than was budgeted for in a particular year, the hospital has to take it on the chin. You do not turn patients away – contractually, you are not allowed to turn patients away, not that you would anyway – but, if it exceeds your budget, it is tough luck, you are not going to get paid any more by the insurer. It is a bit like having a car crash in November or December and finding the insurance company saying 'Sorry, we've had too many crashes this year, we're not going to pay for any more'.

That is the reality of what is happening in private medical insurance. In terms of the consultants, there is actually limited risk for the consultants. There is obviously the cost of medical indemnity, which is a big issue right now. But, in terms of volume risk, there is pretty much none. The consultants are paid for on a fee-per-service basis and there are some restrictions on multiple procedures but it is very much limited. The outpatient charges – some risk is transferred to the patient *via* annual deductibles – which most people will be aware of if they are insured.

THE FUTURE

So what is the future going to look like? Well, before we speculate on what it is going to look like, let us consider what is going to drive change. I think, first, the whole issue of consumer and patient expectations. The Celtic Tiger very definitely has had a dramatic impact here. Patients know what they want. They have good access to information than previously, predominantly via the Internet, and it is quite routine now, say, for a medical oncologist to be confronted by a patient who has been diagnosed with a rare form of cancer and for them to insist on access to a drug that is doing pretty well in a Phase 1 clinical trial in California at the moment – an unproven product, if you like, at this stage. So expectation and information – quite rightly – is increasing. If you like, the shift of power between patient and doctor, and patient and hospital, is definitely moving in the direction of the patient. Not a bad thing.

Private healthcare is becoming more competitive – I think we have seen recently evidence that a number of private hospitals have closed in the last few years, squeezed out by reimbursement rates. We have had St. Gabriel's in Cabinteely, we have had St. Michael's private hospital in Dun Laoghaire, we have had St. Joseph's in Raheny sold to the public sector, we have had Portiuncula in Ballinasloe – and I could go on. The reality is that private hospitals are not a very attractive place to be in, given the power of the purchasers in the market.

Second, you are seeing niche operators arrive on the scene, particularly in areas such as diagnostic facilities, so there are some areas that can be profitable for a nice operator – and those ones are getting picked off by what I would call non-full service operators – whether it is mobile MRI services or a mobile cardiac lab going around the country at the moment. There is really an absence of genuine private medical insurance competition. Restrictions on capacity – any additional capacity that we want to develop has to be approved by the dominant insurer. The harsh reality of it is that margins in private healthcare are being squeezed. A typical margin four or five years ago would have been 20%, ending up with 3% to 6% return on your revenue on the bottom line. That 20% operating margin is down to 15% this year. I am talking about the leading operators in the country. If that continues, then the future is very bleak.

The second group of drivers for change really is the change of focus of religious congregations. Their numbers are declining and, to be honest, many of the religious congregations that got into private healthcare are really questioning whether this is a true part of their mission. So many of them are taking the decision to get out.

The increasing proportion of population insured – we have already seen that 45% of the population are insured; 10 years ago that was about 30% to 31%. The capacity of the public sector – that iss going to be a huge determining factor. If the 3,000 extra beds, and the consultants, and all the other appointments that go with that are actually delivered, then clearly it is going to have an impact on demand for private medical insurance and for access to private hospitals.

There is a culture change towards the public/private mix, I have to say, since the mid-1980s when it was pretty much beyond the pale. Certainly with the creation of the Special Treatment Purchase Fund and with waiting list activity that has gone on over the last number of years, I would have to say that the public sector appears a bit more open to doing a bit more work with the private sector. So, it is all the more surprising then that acute hospitals are left out of the whole prospect of PPP activity going forward.

And then finally there is the ownership and management of the private hospitals – certainly becoming much more commercial, simply because they have to if they are going to survive, and certainly if they are going to meet the expectations of their customers and their patients. Private hospitals, no more than public hospitals, are a people-intensive as well as capital-intensive service. You have got to continually re-invest, if you are to stay ahead in technology.

So, to the future, I really believe that all providers, that all acute hospitals whether public or private, are going to have to transform from an internally-focussed provider culture to a quality customer-led focus. I think the culture is far too 'Aren't you so lucky to have us as a hospital to treat you as a patient?' rather than organising how we do things around the real needs of patients – restructured services on the basis of patient convenience. Five-hour waiting times in Outpatients is outrageous – these would be unacceptable in any other service. If anybody was to go into their bank or a restaurant or any other service place, this would just be totally unacceptable and until hospitals and hospital management, in particular, cop themselves on to realising that this is really their own domain now, we are really going to have severe problems.

Independent accreditation of hospitals is not just a paper exercise. We need independent assessment as to whether we are delivering quality and I am not so sure that the current efforts, welcome though they are, towards accreditation in the public sector, are independent enough. The whole issue of asking the patient and involving the patient in how the place should be run and, finally and ultimately, I think the bottom line is the ultimate problem in the health service right now – there is no accountability. Targets are set and nobody – nobody's career – is truly on the line. In fact, in very many hospitals, the system is almost structured to fail. Each of the individual hospitals is treated as a cost centre, and the best way to come in on target in terms of meeting your costs is to cut service. Whereas, in the private system, if you do not earn next month's income by treating patients, you will not be able to pay next month's wages. The private system is a very different culture – we *need* to treat, the more the merrier and I think that is a fundamental culture shift that has to happen. I am not saying privatise all our public hospitals but management leadership culture change has got to seriously happen if we are going to deliver.

The future of privately funded hospitals will largely be determined by three points. First, we need a competitive stable PMI market – I think we have a stable PMI market right now, but I do not think we have a competitive one. We will need adequate reimbursement levels to sustain technology and investment and to prevent further retrenchment. By any comparison, the reimbursement levels here in Ireland for comparable operations, treatments, diagnoses, etc – are far below international standards. Culturally, that may be a very difficult thing for many people to accept because *via* community rating, private medical insurance has been relatively fairly cheap and that has forced VHI to be very strict in terms of cost control. But, ultimately, if we are to meet the expectations of the patients and the members of VHI and BUPA Ireland, then reimbursement rates are going to have to be corrected, otherwise the private sector is going to go the way of the public.

Finally, government policy in terms of the public/private mix must deliver the public hospital capacity to meet patients needs. So, if the public system investment really does happen and if there is substantial improvement in delivery, then obviously that will have an impact on the future of privately-funded hospitals. I am always amazed at the absence of tax breaks for private hospitals but I think the final point I would make is that there is demand for additional capacity for a new generation of privately-funded hospitals to succeed, but demand in and of itself does not create a market and given the level of investment that is required to provide state-of-the-art private care, building a new hospital from scratch just does not make financial sense and I just do not see new entrants coming into the market. I cannot even see existing players expanding significantly in the market based on the current structure of the industry.

XVII

THE (GREATLY UNDERESTIMATED) COSTS OF FINANCING IRELAND'S UNIVERSITY TEACHING HOSPITALS – WHY IT IS IMPORTANT AND WHAT WE SHOULD BE DOING

TONY MCNAMARA MD

GENERAL MANAGER, CORK UNIVERSITY HOSPITAL, CORK

At the outset, it might be useful to briefly ponder on the title of this presentation, and in particular to focus on the phrase: the (greatly underestimated) costs of financing Ireland's University Training Hospitals (UTHs). There are perhaps two issues contained within this phrase:

- The overt suggestion that the such costs are indeed being continually underestimated

- The possibly somewhat less explicit implication that Ireland's UTHs are indeed being seriously under-financed.

The over-riding suggestion, of course, is more than likely that prolonged and substantially inadequate costing of such key resources has resulted in a persistent level of under-financing for Ireland's UTHs.

The importance of this observation stems from the absolutely central role played by these hospitals in the delivery of our national healthcare services. As well as acting as vital sub-specialist referral centres for a range of illnesses and conditions, particularly within the acute hospital sector, their increasingly diverse and excellent research activities are vitally important in attracting new staff of the highest calibre across the wide spectrum of healthcare personnel.

THE SCOPE OF IRELAND'S UTHs

One simple indicator of the substantial scale of our UTH sector is the number of new admissions to our five medical schools each year. Taking into account all new students – both EU and non-EU, there were 736 admissions in the year 2000. The breakdown of this number by the individual schools was as follows:

TABLE 1: NEW ADMISSIONS TO IRISH MEDICAL SCHOOLS IN 2000

Royal College of Surgeons	265
UCD	206
TCD	110
UCC	90
NUIG	65

Taking into account the very low annual fallout rates from our medical schools, and the five to six-year duration of the undergraduate phase of medical training, there are probably between 3,500 and 4,000 medical students under tuition in our medical schools at any one time. This, of course, is only one component of the overall healthcare training activities associated with our UTHs. In particular, the increasingly academic foundation of nurse training is exerting a major influence on the overall functioning of our UTHs. Likewise, the ever more diverse training needs of a range of associated healthcare professions are frequently either based within, or linked to our medical training centres. Postgraduate training for further professional qualifications such as Memberships, as well as Masters and Doctorate degrees, makes up a final and dramatically expanding layer to the activities of our UTHs.

Indeed, if we accumulate the total number of healthcare-focused students in the overall third-level system, we are likely to arrive at an overall population on the scale of our largest university – University College Dublin.

HAVE THESE CUMULATIVE ACTIVITIES BEEN COSTED ON THE SCALE OF A LARGE UNIVERSITY INSTITUTION?

A recent Medical Council Report provides an insight into the scale of the challenge posed if we aspire to adequately funding medical education in Ireland. Entitled *Review of Medical Schools in Ireland 2001*, the following cost statistics in relation to the average grant for each medical student suggest a major funding deficit:

- The University of Glasgow estimates that the average annual grant for each medical student is €36,430

- Queen's University Belfast receives an annual grant per student of €34,976

- In contrast, Irish medical schools reported that their annual income per medical student was €7,135 to €9,000 (EU students), or €18,665 (non-EU students).

These statistics indicate Irish medical school incomes per student are just 20% to 25% of their Glasgow equivalents for EU students, and 51% for so-called economic fee-paying students. While one could possibly rationalise away a part of these differences, the contrast reflects a serious order of magnitude anomaly in medical education funding in Ireland when compared with two neighbouring teaching institutions.

These brief aggregate statistics indicate a major ongoing funding problem at the core of the training of our healthcare personnel. The obvious questions suggest themselves: what should we do about it? When are we going to make a substantive start in that direction? Furthermore, as we address these questions, it would be fatuous not to recognise the negative change that has occurred in the State's fiscal status in recent times.

WHY ARE WE IN THIS SITUATION, AND WHAT SHOULD WE DO ABOUT IT?

Since an excessive degree of retrospection, or indeed introspection, is unlikely to be very useful, I will address the first part of this question predominantly with a fact-finding rather than recriminatory emphasis. Three possible causative factors come to mind immediately:

- First, until the late 1990s, Irish Exchequer funds had been under severe pressure for more than two decades. Consequently, discretionary additional funding was at a premium over this period, and 'order of magnitude' increases in funding were almost impossible to achieve, other than in the most exceptional of situations.

- Second, the growth of Ireland's medical training infrastructure has been very much incremental, with a gradual improvement of facilities and expansion of service coverage very much the order of the day. Thus, the core of most University medical schools has tended to be traditional departments such as medicine, surgery, obstetrics and gynaecology, and paediatrics while other increasingly vital areas such as oncology, radiotherapy, and geriatrics have only been slowly and often painfully developed

- The final possible explanation for the seemingly yawning gap between Irish and international funding levels for medical education may be the diffusion of our training programmes across five different institutions. In other words, the fact that the overall level in funding was extremely inadequate did not emerge starkly, since it was hidden to a large degree within the discrete management and accounting environments of five independent institutions. Indeed, this remains the situation to a very definite degree today.

CASE HISTORY OF CORK UNIVERSITY HOSPITAL

As an example of the operation of a medical school, I will now briefly discuss my own hospital.

Medical training at Cork University Hospital (CUH) occurs at both undergraduate and postgraduate levels.

Undergraduate training is the responsibility of UCC, which recruits 90 students each year. On completion of their studies, 30 successful students are offered work as Medical Interns in the hospital. During this intern year – which is a prerequisite for formal accreditation as a doctor – interns are paid in full by the hospital, and perform a range of basic medical functions.

One of the recognisable features during this year is the increased demand placed on diagnostic services such as Radiology and Pathology as a direct result of defensive and tentative decision-making by inexperienced interns. The additional cost of this work has, of course, to be met by the hospital, and currently there is no process for the identification and re-imbursement of such costs.

During the intern training year, there is a joint obligation on the Medical School and the hospital to provide the intern with access to training in a variety of medical techniques necessary for the student to progress to the level of Senior House Officer. There are formal quality assurance standards laid down and inspected by the Medical Council.

The second level of medical training is post-graduate, which again is regulated by the Medical Council. The Council exercises this responsibility through training bodies such as the Royal College of Surgeons, the Royal College of Physicians and their various Faculties, Specialist Advisory Committees, and Committees for Higher Training. The standards set by these bodies often carry substantial cost implications in terms of extra staffing, equipment and teaching facilities. Compliance with these standards is mandatory and consequently hospitals are continually open to related inspection.

Needless to say, it is critical that UTHs have their training programmes fully accredited, since failure to do so understandably drastically reduces their attractiveness as a training centre. This places a substantial obligation on the governing body of the hospital to maintain and develop its training environment, and to continue to be at the leading edge in this regard. Non-consultant hospital doctors (NCHDs) are extremely mobile, and will usually not hesitate to move on if they are unhappy with their training facilities.

The structure and delivery of both undergraduate and postgraduate medical training are characterised by the following common features:

- There is no specific mechanism for the identification and quantification of the direct and indirect costs associated with training in UTHs

- The setting of standards is a matter for bodies external to the hospital service. Consequently, norms are applied that have frequently been gestated in other countries with a more highly funded approach to the delivery of training and service

- Until very recently, there has been no mechanism in place in which policy can be developed that recognises the need for a balance to be achieved between training and service provision.

Against this background, it is worth reflecting on the current interface between CUH and UCC in so far as funding for training is concerned.

There are currently 95 consultant medical staff employed in CUH, of whom 15 hold academic contracts with up to 50% of time protected for academic pursuits. The direct pay of a full time academic chair is €150,000 *per annum*, and UCC currently funds the equivalent of six fulltime posts and other positions to a level of approximately €1 million each year.

It is interesting to note that the hospital's annual budget for 2002 is €158 million. This figure is arrived at by the Department of Health & Children (DOHC) substantially on the basis of an annual incremental increase for service development, provision for inflation and various allowances for pay and other known financial contingencies.

The consequence has been that there has been no formal recognition of the need to fund academia through a zero-based budgetary approach, let alone attempt to quantify the respective responsibilities of other bodies such as the Department of Education.

The fact is that, in the absence of such an approach, training has had to develop in a manner that is somewhat secondary to the provision of health service delivery, without any explicit understanding of the optimal mix between service and training.

We must address this fundamental question and structure the funding of hospitals and universities according to what serves both through a dynamic symbiotic relationship.

In the absence of there being a mechanism in place to accurately quantify the costs attributable to training in the hospital, it is difficult to state, with any degree of certainty, the exact contribution that the university makes by way of income to our UTH. While allowances would have to be made for services such as the library, it is unlikely that the overall contribution significantly exceeds 1% of the hospital's annual budget.

This is surely remarkable in a UTH, and no doubt is reflective of the fact that the medical faculty itself is not transparently funded on the basis of the performance of its key function of training medical and nursing staff.

It is almost certain that this apparent disproportionate funding contribution is also a product of a system that has been allowed to develop in a somewhat *ad hoc* basis. Such an approach is, of course, no longer acceptable in terms of accountability, transparency, performance measurement and performance management.

The Medical Faculty at UCC is rapidly expanding beyond the confines of the Schools of Medicine and Dentistry, and now houses a Nursing School with almost 1,200 undergraduate and postgraduate students. Furthermore, approval has been obtained for the establishment of schools of Speech and Language, Pharmacy, and Occupational Health.

The development of these schools for Clinical Support Services follows from the publication of a review of the manpower needs of these services, and they are very important elements of the region's overall healthcare strategy. As part of the support mechanisms being provided to these schools, students will be provided with clinical placements in hospitals and other care settings in adjoining Health Boards.

It is encouraging to see a more pro-active management approach to the implementation of these initiatives, with an agreed structure as regards funding, curriculum content and the identification of opportunities for synergies between the University and Health Boards that strongly contrasts with the medical model that has developed almost by a process of osmosis over the past 150 years.

Indeed, the model for nursing education may well provide a template for other professional training at both undergraduate and postgraduate levels, since there already is a nationally agreed *pro forma* contract that explicitly outlines the obligation on both the University and the employing hospital.

Furthermore, the draft contract provides a structure for payment to trainee nurses for one year of their four-year programme which they will spend in a hospital setting. This provides a much needed transparent and accountable process that will ultimately benefit all parties including the student nurse.

It may well be that this more structured approach to the development of academically-qualified nurses is a consequence of the work of the Commission on Nursing. However, it is to be hoped that it has also evolved because of an appreciation among policy makers of the need to avoid the *ad hoc* approach to the funding and organisation of nurse training that has characterised medical training.

It is worth noting that, in the United Kingdom, there is recognition of the need for a formal contractual arrangement between the health authority and the training body. This is known as the SIFT or Service Increment for Teaching. This obligates both parties to achieve compliance with the provisions of a formal agreement, and it is itself the product of discussion and reflection by both parties on what is in the best interests of their organisations individually and collectively.

THE WAY FORWARD

If we are to make substantive progress in evolving explicit and comprehensive models of cost in terms of our UTHs, and indeed the delivery of healthcare facilities in general, there are a number of vital steps that must be taken.

Step 1: Fully accept the complexity of the contemporary health care environment
Presently, the world of health care services is in a state of extreme and constant flux and change. Unfortunately, our fiscal perspectives are often of necessity dominated by a somewhat stereotypical traditional approach. For example, the vicissitudes of annual budgeting means that senior administrators are constantly faced with the often crude task of cutting expenditure allocations within a constrained time interval, and possibly with insufficient available time to minimise the downside of such a practice. Indeed, the most sophisticated decision-making in terms of 'what precisely to lose, and what precisely to hold' is often taken by local managers far removed from overall planning and decision-making. The ongoing vital challenge of optimising the balance between financial prudence and quality of service can easily be undermined in such circumstances.

Step 2: What are the main components of the health care environment?
In order to make significant inroads in terms of fully understanding the multiplicity of influences within the contemporary healthcare environment, and their actions and interactions, it is vital that we fully accept the multi-disciplinary nature of our enterprise. There is simply no room left for delivery philosophies that are even minutely elitist or isolationist in nature. In turn, the best route towards truly accepting a multidisciplinary approach is to commence with a comprehensive focus on **identifying** the diverse forces impacting on the healthcare system. In this regard, there has been perhaps an inadequate focus on epidemiology in terms of setting the scene by accurately quantifying the needs of the Irish people. Population-based registries in areas such as cancer, suicide, and cerebral palsy are invaluable resources for this vital stage of planning.

While looking at our current saturated acute healthcare system, with demand exceeding capacity in certain instances, one might wonder about the need to worry unduly about quantifying need accurately. However, such an approach can be extremely dangerous and short-sighted, since it can preclude identification of underlying epidemiological trends that predict latent demands for care. Ultimately, we can end up being perplexed by the seemingly endless capacity of the system to alarmingly absorb extra resources, almost indefinitely. As a result, we can have a system that remains in a perpetual state of seeming crisis in terms of demand overload and inadequate delivery capacity. The results can be utterly demoralising for all involved in the operation of the system.

Step 3: Comprehensively parameterise the system

Precisely establishing the expected load on our healthcare system through a combination of detailed evaluation of demographic and epidemiological factors is but the foundation stage in mastering our understanding of cost dynamics. We must also fully quantify the other key components in the system. For example, we require far more detailed rapidly accessible information in terms of the resources that are at our disposal. These notably include staff and detailed infrastructure.

Then when we fully link these two substantial information resources – therapeutic demand AND available infrastructure – we will be able to clearly establish the myriad individual cost components that underlie our services. In the absence of such a detailed, indeed exhaustive, process, we are likely to continue to look at data that may remain over-aggregated, and thus incapable of informing us of the true cost of phenomena such as medical training in our UTHs.

Step 4: Set a realistic time-frame for such work

Thus, the current major lack of detailed fiscal information on the actual financing of our UTHs has resulted largely from encompassing training-related costs within the overall expenditure data. This process has taken place over an extended period of time. Equally, if we are to satisfactorily redress this serious information deficit, a realistic time-frame must be set for doing so.

Step 5: Increased information transparency and availability

If we are to move decisively towards a fully information-resourced healthcare costing environment, there are two particularly important developments required.

First, we must radically improve our ability to translate large volumes of data into usable information that can be employed at the core of a continually evolving decision-making process. Deficiencies in translating data into information occur across both the public and private sectors, and the healthcare sector is certainly no exception. The negative consequences of *lacunae* in this area simply cannot be over-estimated. When one's enterprise is highly diverse in terms of data inputs – as is the case in healthcare delivery – failure to optimise information feedback has a direct, and potentially substantially negative, impact on one's ability to optimise one's planning and operational practices.

So, how do we tackle this major challenge at the centre of our activities in a time of serious data overload? While the answer to this question is neither facile nor brief, I would like to make the following suggestions:

- A good start might be to place a major focus on the problem of comprehensive data management and analysis within the healthcare sector. The days when an over-riding emphasis on the bottom-line sufficed are long gone

- Once the general principle is firmly established, then it is essential that efficient, accessible yet comprehensive data management protocols evolve in order to obviate the need for continually 're-inventing the wheel' across the many organisations involved in the delivery of healthcare in Ireland

- The third point that I would like to stress is the need for far greater sharing of information between the various agencies involved in the delivery of health sector. A culture of openness and transparency in this regard would provide all of us with vital comparative information in order to assess our own performance, and indeed possibly reveal more effective organisational structures and delivery strategies in certain instances.

At the broader level, there is one further vital development required in order to identify and leverage the latent information content of our collective data systems. This of course is the need to fully embed Information Technology-based knowledge management techniques within our policy and decision-making structures. If we truly accept that our work landscape is indeed hugely multi-disciplinary in nature, then we must vigorously adopt all tools and aids that enable us to both fully understand the extremely rich nature of our environment, and to maximise its substantial potential.

FINAL COMMENTS

In conclusion therefore, I would summarise my assessment of the situation in terms of the funding of our UTHs as follows:

- A brief evaluation of comparative funding statistics indicate an extremely low, and unacceptable, level of financing for medical education in Ireland

- This problem affects all partners in the process – the Universities, and the Teaching Hospitals and their umbrella organisations

- Because of the slow incremental nature of the growth of many of our UTHs, there is a severe dearth of specific cost information in relation to the financial demands placed on acute hospitals by their involvement in medical education

- In order to address this *lacuna*, and indeed the wider information needs of our healthcare system, I would strongly recommend a major focus on the need for the development of comprehensive, standardised, and accessible computer-based data management and analytic systems across the entire healthcare spectrum. I believe that it is only in this way that the Irish healthcare infrastructure will be exploited to the full in order to both optimally serve the needs of the population, and provide the highest possible level of value for money to the State.

XVIII

SOME ISSUES IN RISK EQUALISATION IN A COMPETITIVE IRISH HEALTH INSURANCE MARKET

PROFESSOR ALASTAIR WOOD
CHAIRMAN, HEALTH INSURANCE AUTHORITY

I will start by giving some general background. I am going to give a brief history of private health insurance in Ireland, just to fill in some gaps. I want to run through the main features of the present system, and explain concepts such as community rating and risk equalisation. I want to discuss possible forms of instability. I want to outline the statutory role of the Health Insurance Authority, because it is not very well understood and there is a lot of misleading comment in the press about what we are actually supposed to do. Finally, I want to talk about the issues in recommending the introduction or non-introduction of Risk Equalisation – how do we decide whether to recommend to the Minister to bring it in, and at what level should it be. So, these are the topics I will address.

The origins of the PHI market go back to 1957 and the Voluntary Health Insurance Act, which set up VHI. In 1992, the Third Non-Life Directive arrived and, in 1994, the Government allowed for this and gave legislative effect to the principles of open enrolment, lifetime cover, minimum benefit and community rating and allowed for the introduction of risk equalisation. In 1996, the preliminary Risk Equalisation scheme was introduced (see **Slide 1**).

With this new legislation, in 1997, BUPA Ireland entered the Irish market (see **Slide 2**) and, from this time on, the risk equalisation recommendations received significant analysis. One notable part of this was the establishment, by the Minister for Health and Children, of an independent advisory group on risk equalisation chaired by Mr Gerard Harvey. The report of this group is often referred to as the Harvey Report.

In 1999, the then Risk Equalisation Scheme was revoked and a new White Paper was published, based on the Harvey Report. In 2001, the Health Insurance Authority was set up. So we have been in existence for two years and presently we are waiting for the Risk Equalisation recommendations to be laid before Dáil Éireann and the Seanad. We were promised them in March, but because there was an election, the government had other fish to fry. We were told recently it would be before the end of the year, but when it comes in is anybody's guess. But let me stress, until that happens, our hands are tied. We cannot do anything apart from look at the situation in general.

SLIDE 1:

Evolution of Irish Private Health
Insurance 1957-1994

HEALTH INSURANCE

- 1957 Voluntary Health Insurance Act
- 1992 Third Non Life Directive
- 1994 Health Insurance Act
  - Allowed for competition
  - Gave legislative effect to the principals of open enrolment, lifetime cover, minimum benefit and community rating and allowed for the introduction of RE
- 1996 RE Scheme Introduced

SLIDE 2:

Entry of Competition

HEALTH INSURANCE

- 1997 BUPA enters Irish market
- 1998 Harvey Report published
- 1999 Risk Equalisation Scheme Revoked
- 1999 White Paper Published
- 2001 The Health Insurance Authority set up
- 2001 Amendment Act – new RE system
- 2002 RE regulations laid before Dail?

Let me give you the features of the current Irish system (see **Slide 3**). We have what is called "Community Rating". Now this has already been referred to. It is non-discriminatory – you can have a history of disease, you can indulge in all sorts of anti-social activities, you can be of any age – the insurance companies have to charge you the same amount of money. Now, try telling that to your car insurer, that you are not allowed to charge a risk-related premium. Nevertheless, that is what society wants, that is what we have got to honour, and that is what is in the Act. In effect, it amounts to an inter-generational subsidy.

Next, there is 'Open Enrolment'. Private health insurance companies cannot turn anyone away. If someone comes along, no matter if he is coughing and wheezing, they must take him and charge him the same premium as everybody else. So that is open enrolment – cover is open to everyone except the over-65s. You cannot take out private medical insurance for the first time if you are over 65.

SLIDE 3:

Features of Current Irish System

...HEALTH
INSURANCE

- Community rating – non-discriminatory, premium rates not risk related – in effect an inter-generational cross-subsidy
- Open enrolment – cover open to all except over 65s
- Lifetime cover – continuity of cover irrespective of onset of illness or claims record - existing subscribers cannot be discontinued
- Minimum benefits

In Ireland, we also have 'Lifetime Cover' – continuity of cover irrespective of history of illness or claims record. You cannot be discontinued – it is unlike car insurance again. If you cause a big pile-up on the motorway or something like that, your car insurer probably would want to double your premium. VHI or BUPA Ireland cannot do that, it is not allowed.

Finally, there is a level of minimum benefits set out in the Act, but in view of our time constraints, I will not go into these in too much detail.

Community rating is a very fine concept (see **Slide 4**). It makes sure that everybody pays the same for health insurance, no matter their condition, no matter their background, no matter what genes they inherited from their parents. We are all in the same boat together, everyone is going to get looked after. It is admirable.

But if you look at it, you have this phenomenon of consumers selecting against the system. The reason for this is that, because there is this single community rate, health insurance is relatively cheap in Ireland. Well, it is if you are aged 65. You are getting a tremendous bargain. But if you are aged 25, you are probably paying two or three times more than you need to. This is the problem. In a sense, this single community rate amounts to a subsidy from the young to the old. That is essentially what is happening.

Now, if insurers' risk profiles differ significantly, there is potential for other difficulties to arise, such as those arising from predatory pricing (which I will explain in a moment) and price-following. These are probably familiar terms to those in the audience from the insurance industry; probably less familiar though to clinicians and hospital managers. So let me go into this a little bit.

SLIDE 4:

Vulnerability of Community Rating

- Consumers selecting against the system
- If insurers' risk profiles differ significantly there is potential for other difficulties to arise such as those resulting from
  - Predatory Pricing and
  - Price Following

This next slides (**Slide 5** and **5a**) show an interesting graph – risk against age.

SLIDE 5:

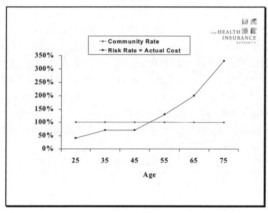

SLIDE 5A

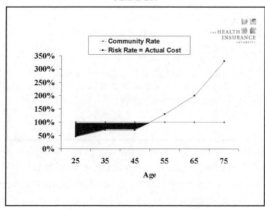

Now, as you can see this is the percentage risk per member of an insurance scheme. So if you are aged 25, you are at 50% on the graph, whereas if you are aged 75, you are at 350%. So, basically, your risk of making a claim is very low down when you are young, and then it grows exponentially with age. This is what I mean when I say that young people are paying a lot more for their insurance than they need to. It is only really when you get to the age of 50 that you start to get your money's worth, as it were, out of Private Medical Insurance.

In a sense, the whole process of community rating depends on inter-generational solidarity. The young are paying more, so that they will be looked after when they grow old. The trouble with this of course is that a lot of the young look at this and think, 'This is a mug's game'. I have an acquaintance who has only recently taken out insurance in her late-40s and I said to her, 'You're freeloading', and she said 'No, at all. I've got it all worked out' and she got away with it. She didn't have any serious illness and she has saved pots of money. Now if everyone did this, the whole system of private medical insurance would collapse. That is one problem.

Now, to discourage people like my colleague, various changes are being considered and the Department of Health & Children has asked for our opinion on this (**Slide 6**). We have consulted widely and we are about to submit a response to them. What we are looking at, first of all, is that people currently insured should not be affected. But late entrants should pay a loading on the community rate. That would put a stop to someone who thinks, 'My chance of requiring hospitalisation for a major procedure under the age of 50 is pretty small. I'm going to take a chance on that – I'm not going to join until I'm older.'

SLIDE 6:

Change Community Rating?

                                                             the HEALTH
                                                             INSURANCE
                                                             authority

- Individual risk rate < community rate up to age 50 – discourages young entrants
- People currently insured not affected
- Late entrants should pay loadings on standard community rates
- Underpins stability and encourages earlier entry - "inter-generational trust"
- Credits for previous cover

So we think that it might be better if the rate at which you pay depended on your age at joining, meaning people who joined for the first time at age 40 or 50 would be paying a much higher rate than those people who joined at 25. This would underpin stability and encourage inter-generational trust. There are some grey areas: What do you do with people who move into the State? Something like 5% of our population are non-Irish nationals – provision would have to be made for them – but that's the general idea.

I want to talk a bit now about risks. In the context of open enrolment and lifetime cover, how can risks be separated? (see **Slide 7**) There is certainly evidence that new health insurance consumers are likely to be younger. There is also evidence to suggest that younger people are more likely to switch insurers. This happens in a lot of services – in financial services, mobile phone take-up – younger people are more likely to switch to a new provider. Older people, perhaps, do not like to change – although there is no reason they should feel this way, as under open enrolment they can change at any time.

SLIDE 7:

Separation of Risks

…HEALTH
INSURANCE

- In the context of Open Enrolment and Lifetime
  Cover, how can risks be separated?
  – New health insurance consumers are likely to
    be younger.
  – There is evidence to suggest that younger
    people are more likely to switch insurer.
  – Cream Skimming is still possible.

Cream-skimming is also possible, even under community rating. 'Cream-skimming', I should explain, is an insurance term for targeting particularly advantageous groups of consumers. It is a bit like cherry-picking; you look for the people who are low risk. So, motor insurers might try to get female drivers over 35, but would run a mile from men under 30. The same thing can happen in the health insurance industry, even under community rating. Selective advertising – offering packages linked to services used mainly by low risk individuals. If you offer very good maternity cover, it is going to make your offering much more attractive to people who are low risk than to people who are past child-bearing age. That is just one example. You can also structure the product so that the plans are more attractive to low risk consumers. In other countries, there has been a history of direct mailing to healthy districts – insurers know the postcodes and the zipcodes that correspond to where the affluent people live, and they target these areas. So that is one problem.

SLIDE 8:

Predatory Pricing

- An insurer with a much lower risk profile chooses to charge a much lower premium
- This insurer might primarily attract lower risk customers from the other insurers
- Average claim of other insurers may then increase forcing an increase in premiums
- Cycle continues
- Insurers may be forced out of the market
- Such market instability is not in consumers' interests

Another problem is predatory pricing. The scenario here is that an insurer with a significantly lower risk profile chooses to charge a significantly lower premium. That insurer is experiencing a much lower claims cost. Now, there is some anecdotal evidence that, of the two insurers in Ireland, one has a much older client base than the other. We will not know the exact figures on this until the regulations are passed and we can collect data from all the clients. So expect good reports from us, once we can get this data. But this seems to be primarily what is happening.

So this insurer might primarily attract lower-risk clients from the other insurer. The other insurer – with more old people – finds itself with an even bigger percentage of old people and has to increase its premiums even further (because these people are making more expensive claims). So, even more people go over to the other insurer. And this goes on. And, if you have more than two insurers in the market, it becomes very complicated – it becomes very difficult to describe. So this cycle continues until such a time as an insurer may be forced out of the market.

Such market instability is certainly not in the consumer's interest. It may undermine confidence in private medical insurance of any kind to such an extent that people just opt out of it completely. That would be a very bad scenario in regard to the provision of extra capacity funded by PMI.

A second way in which the system can be abused is the system of price following (see **Slide 9**). An insurer with a much lower risk profile chooses to charge a *slightly* lower premium than its competitors. Now, I emphasise the 'slightly' – the slightly cheaper premium attracts younger clients and corporate clients. If you are somebody like Intel and you have 1,500 workers insured with one insurance company, and you are paying the bill, and another insurance company offers you a reduction of even 5%, youare going to go with that. But if you are an older person, paying independently, you will probably stay put. So, the lower premium attracts some low-risk members from competitors, but it does not attract too many high-risk members. This again forces the competitor with the high-risk members to increase premiums. The insurer with the lower-risk profile adjusts its premium to just below the higher premium – again there is a flow of the less risky clients from the first insurer and the whole cycle continues.

What happens here is very much against the interests of the consumer. It results in all consumers paying the premium suitable to the highest risk profile. So, again, we are left with a situation where one insurer may end up with all the high-risk people, and the other insurer or insurers may end up with all the low-risk people. This is a situation that gives rise to instability.

SLIDE 9:

> ... HEALTH INSURANCE
>
> ## Price Following
>
> - An insurer with a much lower risk profile chooses to charge a slightly lower premium than its competitors
> - The lower premium attracts some lower risk members from the competitors but avoids attracting too many high risk members
> - This forces competitors to increase premiums, the insurer with the lower risk profile follows the increase and the cycle continues
> - Results in all consumers paying the premium suitable to the highest risk profiles

SLIDE 10:

> ... HEALTH INSURANCE
>
> ## Risk Equalisation
>
> - Risk equalisation is a process that aims to equitably neutralise differences in insurers' costs due to variations in the health status of their members.
> - Which risk factors do we include? Age and sex seem essential. What about lifestyle or other factors such as smoking, obesity, skiing or social class.
> - Could utilisation capture these other factors?

Risk Equalisation is a process that aims to neutralise differences in insurer's costs due to variations in the health status of their members. Already I have used age as a measure of health status, but what other factors could be included? Age and sex seem important. Lifestyle could be important. Obesity. Engaging in winter sports – a lot of hospitalisation results from people involved in tobogganing and skiing. Class is also a factor, as everyone knows. The answer is, nobody seems to include these in any country – they are just too difficult to measure. It is possible that utilisation of services could capture some of these other factors, but the Chief Executive of the Midlands Health Board in his paper made an appeal for much better Information Technology and that would certainly measure things like utilisation. At the moment, even within the public system, different hospitals have different ways of doing it. In the private system, the different hospitals are more concerned with accounting than with actual procedures.

Here's a very simple example of Risk Equalisation (**Slides 11 and 12**). Suppose Insurer A has average claims costs of 140, of which 90 is due to risk factors and 50 is due to other factors – administration costs. Insurer B has average claims costs of 70, of which 40 is due to risk factors. Now, assuming we can isolate the claims costs relating to risk factors, and assuming the insurers are roughly the same size, risk equalisation would equalise these costs at 65 for each insurer. So it is the costs that arise from risk factors that are equalised – *not* the administration costs. If one insurer is relatively more efficient than the other, they should be allowed to retain the benefit of their efficiency.

SLIDE 11:

Simple example of RE

- Insurer A has average claim costs of 140 of which 90 is due to risk factors and 50 to other factors (e.g. administration costs)
- Insurer B has average claim costs of 70 of which 40 is due to risk factors
- Assuming that we can isolate the claim costs relating to risk factors, RE would equalise these costs (at 65 for each insurer) and leave the other claim costs unchanged.

SLIDE 12:

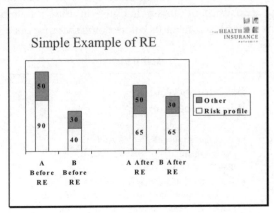

I want to turn now to the Health Insurance Authority and exactly what we do (see **Slide 13**). The Authority has many roles; one of the key ones is in recommending to the Minister whether Risk Equalisation should be commenced. Now, this role differs at three levels of risk difference between the health insurers.

SLIDE 13:

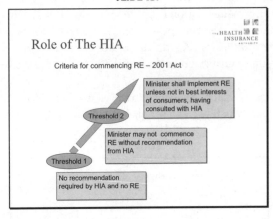

Below Threshold 1 – nobody does anything, no recommendation is required from the Authority and no Risk Equalisation scheme is implemented.

There is a second threshold, which is higher. Again, these are in the recommendations to be laid before the Houses of the Oireachtas and we cannot confirm what they are. But Threshold 2 is likely to be considerably higher than Threshold 1. The Minister may not commence Risk Equalisation without the recommendation of the Health Insurance Authority. Now, this is contrary to what is often said in the press. The Minister does not have the power to introduce Risk Equalisation on his own, unless Threshold 2 is passed, in which case the Minister can say 'I think the situation is so bad that I'm going to implement risk equalisation, unless it's not in the best interests of the consumer'. He is obliged to consult us before doing that, but not to listen to us.

SLIDE 14:

Basis for the Authority's
Recommendation

- 2001 Act stipulates that the Authority considers the best overall interests of health insurance consumers.
- These interests include "the need to maintain the application of community rating across the market for health insurance and to facilitate competition".

If the Minister commences a Risk Equalisation Scheme, then the Authority will be responsible for the administration of the scheme. It is we who will calculate the transfers and operate the fund that will pay and receive contributions. Now, the basis for our recommendation is set down in the 2001 Act. It states that the Authority shall consider the best overall interests of Health Insurance consumers. These interests include the rather contradictory requirements of retaining community rating across the health insurance market, and facilitating competition.

We have already made our preliminary views (see **Slide 15**) known in a consultative paper, which you can see on our website (http://www.hia.ie).

SLIDE 15:

Preliminary views of the
Authority

- Difficulties can arise for a CR market when risk profiles differ significantly.
- Therefore, the introduction of RE could be justified in the appropriate circumstances.
- However, the introduction of RE may not always be appropriate and could potentially do harm.
- The Authority will be mindful of the effect on competition.

We believe that difficulties can arise for a community-rated market when risk profiles differ significantly. We believe that the introduction of Risk Equalisation could be justified in appropriate circumstances. However, the introduction of Risk Equalisation may not always be appropriate and could potentially do harm, and we will be mindful of the effect on the competition in making any recommendations to the Minister.

Just to conclude, these are some issues that we will be considering in reaching our decision (see **Slide 16**). When the regulations are introduced, we will consider the differences in risk profiles. We will consider the relative sizes of the insurers. The percentage of coverage has increased; the percentage of people with private health insurance in Ireland is now at very close to 50%. The other factor is that BUPA Ireland has been making further inroads into the market, so the situation is not as unbalanced as it was. We will look at the age/sex profile of the major insurers – this again is related to the risk. The commercial status of insurers – there is a difference between a private company, and a State company that is owned by the Minister for Health & Children. The HIA needs to ensure a level playing field. We will look at the rate of premium inflation – we will look at what price rises the various insurers have had over the past few years. We will also look at the numbers of insurers, and the numbers of new entrants.

SLIDE 16:

Some issues to be considered   the HEALTH INSURANCE AUTHORITY

- Differences in risk profiles,
- Relative sizes of insurers,
- Age / sex profiles of insurers' members,
- Commercial status of insurers,
- Rate of premium inflation,
- Number of insurers / new entrants,
- Effect of any transfer on premiums,
- Size of the market and
- Effect on the business plans / solvency of insurers.

Again, I have a lot of sympathy with the view that more insurers in the market would increase stability. I actually privately believe – this is *not* a Health Insurance Authority view – that more insurers make a more stable market. We will also look at the effect of any transfer on the premium – if we transfer too much from one company to another, then it might be that a company that has to make a big payment then has to put up its premiums by a large amount. We will look at the size of the market, and also we will look at the effect on the business plans and the solvency of the insurers. It would help nobody if one of the big insurers were to go bust – it would completely destroy confidence in the market.

XIX

RES – IMPACT ON COMPETITION IN THE IRISH PMI MARKET: PERSPECTIVES FROM A EUROPEAN & GLOBAL INSURER

AIDAN CASSELLS
DEPUTY GROUP CHIEF EXECUTIVE, AXA INSURANCE

I listened with great interest to Professor Wood's presentation and I must say that I sympathise with him in trying to manage this very complex area.

To some extent, having listened to the earlier contributions about the financial challenges and the social issues facing us in the health service, I feel a little inadequate talking about the rather narrower issue of insurance and how we can increase competition in the Private Medical Insurance (PMI) market. However, Mark Moran's paper gave me some sort of hope that there is a role for the private sector in making a contribution to the efficiency and effectiveness of the health sector generally, provided we can get the model right.

So I am going to give you a somewhat narrow perspective from a private insurer on the PMI market we have today and the difficulties we face in promoting genuine competition in this critical sector. I will also give you a brief European perspective on it, because I chair the Single Market Committee of the Comité Europeén des Assurances (European insurance committee), which is very involved in the current debate on completing the European Financial Services Marketplace. Coincidentally health insurance is actually a live issue in Europe at the moment, so I have some insights from a European perspective that may be of interest.

I want to start, however, by looking at PMI from a purely local insurance perspective. By any standards, the PMI market in Ireland is a very highly regulated market and it looks as if we are about to increase that regulation through the introduction of risk equalisation. That is going to make the job of promoting competition in the health insurance sector in Ireland extremely difficult, if not impossible, going forward – it is a huge issue and challenge for those wishing to modernise our market

It is important to recall also that uncertainty surrounding RES was also a major barrier to market entry. In AXA, we looked at the health insurance market five years ago – around the time BUPA Ireland came in – and our biggest concern, and the reason we ultimately decided not to enter the market, was uncertainty surrounding future introduction and financial impact of RES. Whilst clarity on the future of risk equalisation is going to be helpful, if it is the wrong kind of clarity – the introduction of RES – it will probably be the final nail in the coffin of a competitive PMI market. That is a personal view, and some of you will disagree fundamentally with me on that point.

One of the key questions in relation to the regulatory environment for health insurance is how policymakers arrived at the conclusion that PMI is so fundamentally different from other forms of insurance to justify such a regulatory approach that is out of step with local and European insurance norms.

Before trying to answer this question, we should consider why most of us buy PMI in Ireland. PMI should really be purchased to reimburse the cost of healthcare (a visit to a hospital or a doctor, etc.) but most of these costs are already covered under the basic social welfare system which we all pay handsomely for through the tax system. In reality, therefore, for many of us, PMI is really purchased to provide a higher standard of accommodation in a hospital rather than enhanced medical treatment, and selfishly to allow us jump the queue on everybody else.

These are the factors that drive many of us to take out health insurance. Is that form of insurance so sociably more desirable than providing for your pension? Providing for the death of your spouse or a family member? Taking out car insurance, which is compulsory to compensate road accident victims? Is it really so different that we have to build this unique regulation system for this one type of insurance?

I am not convinced (I never have been convinced and you will find it very hard to ever convince me) that there is a logical reason why we need this type of regulation for a form of insurance which is purely to provide the well-off with a facility to buy a particular type of care when they go into hospital, which is usually unrelated to the medical treatment they get. So I have a fundamental issue with the need to have a special regulatory structure for health insurance in Ireland.

We are totally out of step with Europe – Europe is deregulating everywhere unless there are cogent reasons to maintain costly regulations that invariably (as in the case in Ireland) act as real barriers to market entry. That is the way of the future, whether we like it or not. We are totally out of line with the Government's own policy and the OECD Report on regulation which says that the only effective way to run an economy and public services is through increased competition and deregulation (getting rid of unnecessary regulation). Ireland is going the other way, uniquely, on health insurance, which is interesting.

That leads me – and many of my colleagues in the insurance industry – to a strong suspicion that the regulatory environment that has evolved around health insurance since 1995 is designed not to open up and remove the VHI monopoly, but is rather designed to protect the State-owned government monopoly without any genuine concern about the consumer agenda. The consumer is often used by both private sector and public sector as a means to introduce or maintain regulations to protect the *status quo* rather than from any genuine concern for the consumer.

There is a concern that has been voiced by many of us about the sustainability of the relationship between Government as regulator and owner of the major company in the PMI market I wonder, if we look at the deregulation of the telecoms sector and other sacred cows that existed in the past, whether we would have made the significant strides that we have made in deregulation of those public utilities over the past 10 years if we approached them in the same way we are attempting to deregulate the health insurance sector. I doubt it very much.

I have a fundamental question mark over the interpretation of Article 54, of the 1992 TNLD, which forms the basis for the Regulation that was brought in here for the health insurance sector. Article 54, by exception, allows Member States to maintain local regulatory controls on health insurance products, (which in our case involves restrictions on product design, pricing, etc,), where the health insurance product is a partial or complete alternative to the cover provided by the social security system. The PMI system in Ireland is neither a partial nor complete alternative to our national health system, which is open to all citizens with few exceptions. In Ireland, we all pay our taxes, and we have full cover under the state system. What we buy, through PMI, is a total discretionary and voluntary cover that allows us a higher standard of accommodation when we go into hospitals, and to jump the queue on our other colleagues.

I would not like to be making the case before the European Court – and it will end up there eventually – to say that our system is such that it complies with the regulations to allow us to actually do what we are doing. I believe there will be a fundamental challenge to our PMI system under European Law in the not too distant future.

Looking to the future, one of the issues I have with our system at the moment is about the 'sacred cow' called 'community rating'. In many respects, it is the foundation on which the whole regulatory monster we have created is based. I do not accept that somebody who has a lifestyle who exposes them to higher risk, be it in relation to drinking, drugs or whatever, should pay the same premium as someone with a much lower risk lifestyle. I would not want to argue for this approach in any other form of insurance, be it motor insurance, home insurance, or public liability insurance. The whole principle of private insurance is based on philosophy of risk differentiation, which allows for a fairer and more equitable basis for distributing the cost of claims among the insured population. Again, I do not accept the logic that health insurance is so unique and sociably desirable that we have to maintain this unique system of community rating.

Bear in mind that community rating was only introduced in 1994 – it was not a feature of our system before then. Again, I would fundamentally question community rating as a viable long-term basis for health insurance in Ireland if – and it is a big if – if you want a competitive insurance market. It would be extremely difficult to do that if we maintain community rating and at the same time bring in risk equalisation and maintain the other factors that make Ireland extremely unattractive to any private insurer. There is a real risk that the introduction of risk equalisation will force out the only competitor in the market – BUPA Ireland. I think that is a greater risk to the stability of the marketplace than moving towards a more open and competitive market place based on the regulatory principles and philosophy that underlies the new European approach to the Single Market.

What do I think is the way forward? Do not introduce risk equalisation. I think you are going to have fundamental problems in Europe if you persist in so doing. I think if it fails in Europe, we have got to have a Plan B. I believe our Plan B should involve going back to what probably should have been done in the first place, which is to look at a sensible migration away from the current PMI model, towards a an open and competitive private insurance system based on the principles that seem to work well in most other European countries.

The industry, and most logical people, would say that we need time to migrate from where we are today to the new system. I suggest with respect that our efforts should be put to trying to come up with a more sustainable long-term system that will promote competition, than to try to build a huge regulatory environment to maintain a structure that is probably not viable for very much longer.

This is a problem that could confront us very quickly, given the current direction in Europe as a whole. So, that is a fairly quick summary, but that is essentially the message I want to give. I think our PMI system is fundamentally flawed, it does not allow competition in the health insurance market in Ireland, and I think we have got to evolve Plan B fairly quickly.